A Portrait of

Paul

Making disciples of all nations

David J. Valleskey

Northwestern Publishing House
Milwaukee, Wisconsin

Second printing, 2004

Cover illustration is by Frank Ordaz.

Library of Congress Control Number 2002101112
Northwestern Publishing House
1250 N. 113th St., Milwaukee, WI 53226-3284
© 2002 by Northwestern Publishing House
http://www.wels.net
Published 2002
Printed in the United States of America
ISBN 0-8100-1323-1

Contents_____

Preface _____

IT WOULD BE DIFFICULT to overestimate the importance of the role of the apostle Paul in the fulfillment of Christ's commission to make disciples of all nations, even though Paul himself would be the first to exclaim, "Who am I that you should be spending so much time talking about me?" "I am the least of the apostles," he told the Corinthians, "and do not even deserve to be called an apostle, because I persecuted the church of God" (1 Corinthians 15:9). "I was once a blasphemer and a persecutor and a violent man," he reminded Timothy (1 Timothy 1:13). He told the Corinthians, "By the grace of God I am what I am" (1 Corinthians 15:10). To the Romans he wrote: "I glory in Christ Jesus in my service to God. I will not venture to speak of anything except what Christ has accomplished through me in leading the Gentiles to obey God" (Romans 15:17,18).

A study of the life and ministry of Saint Paul is really a celebration of the saving grace of God in Christ. It is a testimony to what God can do when he applies the benefits of Christ's finished work to an individual and then calls and equips him for service. If we keep these truths in mind, we will not embarrass Paul by unduly praising him and his work. "Whatever you do," even when you study Paul, "do it all for the glory of God" (1 Corinthians 10:31).

Having said that, we must also say that not every Christian is a Paul. Though all Christians are equal heirs of salvation, not all Christians are equally gifted. In Romans chapter 12 and 1 Corinthians chapter 12, Paul speaks about various gifts that the

Spirit of God graciously grants to members of the body of Christ. Even a brief perusal of these gifts reveals that Paul was blessed with most of them. He was an apostle. He was a gifted preacher, teacher, leader, and administrator. He was an evangelist. He was a worker of miracles. He spoke in tongues. God intended to accomplish great things through Paul; therefore he blessed him singularly with the multiplicity of gifts needed to carry out the mission committed to him.

To think of what God accomplished through Paul in just a few short years boggles the mind. In about ten years' time (A.D. 47–57), God used Paul to establish churches in at least four provinces of the Roman Empire—Galatia, Asia, Macedonia, and Achaia—very likely also in Syria, Cilicia, and Illyricum, so that Paul could say, "From Jerusalem all the way around to Illyricum, I have fully proclaimed the gospel of Christ" (Romans 15:19). At no time before or after has the church expanded so rapidly and into so many cultures in such a short time.

Then there are Paul's writings. Thirteen letters, one-fourth of the content of the New Testament, came from his pen. These letters contribute the lion's share of our understanding of the message of Christianity, especially of the cardinal doctrine of justification by God's grace through faith in Jesus.

It is this Paul, by the grace of God a missionary *par excellence* and by the inspiration of the Spirit the author of key books of the New Testament, who will occupy our attention in this study. Our focus will not be so much on the theology of Paul, though one can hardly avoid discussing Paul's theology when one studies Paul, as it will be on Paul's missionary methodology.

The first of the five parts takes a brief look at the times in which Paul lived. The second and third parts follow a chronological pattern, reviewing Paul's early years and his journeys and giving special attention to what we can discern of Paul's mission strategy. Part 4 centers our thoughts on characteristics of Paul's missionary message. Finally, Part 5 looks at Paul's method of follow-up—how he prepared his congregations to get along without him and also to become parents of other congregations.

Part One _____

The Times in Which Paul Lived

"WHEN THE TIME HAD FULLY COME," Paul writes, "God sent his Son" (Galatians 4:4). It was not only the fullness of time for the coming of the Messiah. It was also the fullness of time for the proclamation of the message about the Messiah who did come in fulfillment of God's promise. In a marvelous way the Lord saw to it that the times were right. Our prayer to God for the church—"Let nothing hinder your Word from being freely proclaimed to the joy and edifying of Christ's holy people"—was a blessed reality in Paul's day to a degree never realized before or since.

The Diaspora

There was first of all the Jewish Diaspora, the scattering of the Jewish people from their homeland. It began when they were deported by their enemies, the Assyrians and Babylonians, in 722 and 586 B.C. The descendants of the Jewish captives in Assyria became a part of the Diaspora, as did the descendants of the large number of Jews in Babylon who chose not to return to their homeland when Cyrus reversed the policy of Nebuchadnezzar and permitted transplanted people to go home.

It is likely that the Jewish synagogue came into existence during the time of the exile, as an attempt to preserve the Torah in the midst of a pagan environment. The synagogue served a valuable purpose in the spread of the gospel in the Mediterranean world. With the presence of synagogues in most major communities, the message of the Old Testament—its monotheism, its strong moral code, and its messianic prophecies—preceded the arrival of Paul. The ability to begin his ministry in a synagogue, which he did on almost every occasion, gave Paul an advantage that many a missionary today doesn't have. He had a nucleus of people who already knew much of the truth, who now simply needed to be pointed to Jesus as the fulfillment of the messianic promise. The synagogues afforded Paul a series of advanced posts from which he could preach the gospel.

Those who have sought to begin mission work in areas where no churches exist know what a blessing it is to have a small nucleus as a base of operations. It's a privilege to gain a foothold in a particular area through that nucleus. It was the same with Paul. One might have thought that after several attempts, he would have discontinued his practice of going first to the synagogue, since the results were hardly encouraging. But, in addition to the fact that he dearly loved his fellow Jews, Paul saw it as a good way by which to get his foot in the door of a community. That this was also the approach the Lord wanted him to take appears to be indicated in Romans 1:16, where Paul describes the gospel as "the power of God for the salvation of everyone who believes: first for the Jew, then for the Gentile."

The relatively loose structure of the synagogue permitted Paul to make maximum use of it as his launch pad for the gospel. Since the synagogues did not have full-time preachers, any capable adult Jewish male might be invited to lead the worship. With his background Paul made an ideal "guest preacher." Luke makes it clear that this was Paul's general practice when, in describing Paul's and Barnabas' early work in Iconium, he says that they went *"as usual* into the Jewish synagogue. There they spoke" (Acts 14:1, italics added).

Another way by which God prepared the world for the missionary work of Paul was through the migration of Jews to Egypt. During the time of the Babylonian captivity, some Jews, in fear of the Babylonians and in defiance of the Lord, had settled in both Lower and Upper Egypt (Jeremiah 43–46). Migration accelerated from the third century B.C. on, following the death of Alexander the Great, during the time that Egypt (and often Palestine) was under the control of the Ptolemies. Alexandria especially, founded in 331 B.C. by Alexander the Great, became the home of a large number of Jews. Two of its five quarters were inhabited chiefly by Jews. The Jewish historian Philo reports that about one million Jews were living in Egypt, about a seventh or an eighth of the whole population, a percentage exceeded only in Syria, where over a million Jews lived in the midst of a somewhat smaller population.[1]

Alexandria was a Greek city. The culture was Greek. The language was Greek. The Jews, as they became involved in the trade and business of the city, naturally began to use the Greek language themselves. This in time reduced the Hebrew language to a seldom-employed vehicle of communication apart from its use in the synagogue. It was apparently in response to the need for a Bible in the language of the people that the Septuagint (LXX), a Greek version of the Hebrew Bible, was translated, possibly during the reign of Ptolemy II Philadelphus (284–247 B.C.).

The Septuagint became the Bible of the Diaspora, or at least it found a use alongside the Hebrew text. Paul uses it extensively when quoting the Old Testament in his epistles. In about half of his Old Testament quotes, he uses the exact wording of the Septuagint. But even more important for Paul's missionary work is the fact that the use of the Septuagint in the worship of the synagogue would make it possible for non-Hebrew-speaking Gentiles to participate in the synagogue worship. On his first missionary journey, for example, when Paul was given the opportunity in the synagogue at Antioch of Pisidia to speak a "message of encouragement," he was able to direct his address to both the "men of Israel" and "you Gentiles who worship God" (Acts 13:15,16). These Gentiles almost certainly would not have been there had the worship been conducted solely in a language they could not understand. When Paul was no longer permitted to speak in the synagogue, it appears that this group of

"God-fearing Gentiles" (Acts 13:26) left with him to form the nucleus of the Christian church in Antioch (Acts 13:48). The same thing happened in other places in the course of Paul's journeys, for example, Thessalonica (Acts 17:1-4).

There was movement of Jews not only from west to east and east to west, but also during the time of Seleucus I (358–280 B.C.), another of the successors of Alexander the Great, many Jews migrated north to Syria, chiefly to Antioch but also to Damascus. From there they traveled still farther north, to Cilicia and Galatia, and then west into the cities of the provinces of Asia, Macedonia, and Achaia. Josephus tells us that Seleucus settled many Jews in cities that he founded in Asia and lower Syria and then conferred rights of citizenship upon them.[2]

After Pompey and the Roman armies conquered Palestine around 60 B.C., the dispersion of the Jews gradually reached to the western end of the Roman Empire. Pompey took some to Rome as slaves. By New Testament times, more Jews were living outside of Palestine than within it. Estimates of the number of Jews living in the Diaspora range from three to seven million. Strabo, the Greek geographer, writes about them: "Now these Jews have already gotten into all cities; and it is hard to find a place in the habitable earth that hath not admitted this tribe of men, and is not possessed by them."[3] The Alexandrian Jew Philo quotes a letter from Herod Agrippa I (A.D. 37–44) to the Emperor Caligula in which he sought religious and civic freedom for the Jews in Cilicia, Pamphylia, Asia all the way to Bithynia, and also Thessaly, Boetia, Macedonia, and the city of Corinth. By Paul's day, then, Jews were living in virtually every part of the Mediterranean world, primarily in the cities, where they engaged in business and trade.

The practical benefit to Paul of this migration to the north and the west is not difficult to see. Where the Jews went, their synagogues went and with that an opportunity for Paul to proclaim the gospel to the Jews. But not only to the Jews. Paul generally found Gentiles in the synagogues as well as Jews, for many of the Jews of the Diaspora, especially of the pharisaical persuasion, were evangelistic in their own right. Recall Jesus' words "Woe to you, teachers of the law and Pharisees, you hypocrites! You travel over land and sea to win a single convert, and when he becomes one, you make him twice as much a son of hell as you are" (Matthew 23:15). Though the message they brought as they sought to win proselytes was far from a perfect one, they did proclaim the Bible's message that there is no God but one, that all the gods of the nations are idols, that the Lord and the Lord alone made the heavens, and that he alone is worthy of our worship. This was helpful preparation for Paul's visits. When he entered a heathen city, he could know that there were already some among the Gentiles who had been brought to a conviction that idolatry was folly, that the God of the Old Testament is the one true God. He could build on that by pointing to the one true God's covenant promises and the fulfillment of those promises in Jesus of Nazareth.

We see the gracious hand of the Lord at work here. It was for only a relatively brief period of time when Jews felt the kind of openness to foreigners and things foreign that brought Gentiles into the synagogue. Harnack writes:

> The keener the opposition within Palestine to the foreign dominion, and the nearer the great catastrophe came [the destruction of Jerusalem], the more strenuous grew the reaction against all that was foreign, as well as the idea that whatever was un-Jewish would perish in the judgment. Not long before the destruction of Jerusalem, in all probability, the controversy between the schools of Hillel [who spoke out in favor of propagating the faith] and Shammai ended in a complete victory for the latter. Shammai was not indeed an opponent of the mission in principle, but he subjected it to the most rigorous conditions. . . . Intercourse with the pagans was confined within the strictest of regulations, and had to be given up as a whole.[4]

Another way by which the Lord used the Diaspora for his purposes is seen by the status of *religio licita* (lawful religion) granted to the Jewish religion. Josephus informs us that it was Julius Caesar (died 44 B.C.) who gave to the Jews of the empire a guarantee that they could practice their religion freely. He also granted them exemption from military service and the right to collect the annual temple tax.[5] The early Christian church came to share in this benefit through the decree of Gallio, who served as proconsul of Achaia approximately A.D. 51–52. When the Jews of Corinth brought Paul into court, they charged him:

"This man . . . is persuading the people to worship God in ways contrary to the law."

Just as Paul was about to speak, Gallio said to the Jews, "If you Jews were making a complaint about some misdemeanor or serious crime, it would be reasonable for me to listen to you. But since it involves questions about words and names and your own law—settle the matter yourselves. I will not be a judge of such things." (Acts 18:13-15)

By this action Gallio in effect declared the Christian religion to be nothing more than an offshoot, or sect, of Judaism. Thus Christianity was brought under the same protective umbrella as Judaism.

The privileged position that Judaism enjoyed, and with it Christianity, was not to last forever. In A.D. 70 Vespasian put an end to the legal existence of a separate Jewish nation and merged it into the general population.[6] But this did not occur until the first major thrust of Christianity into the world through Paul was completed, another example of the way God arranged everything in such a way as to assure an initial unencumbered spread of the gospel.

Greek culture

A second major aspect of God's preparation of the world for the advance of the gospel through Paul and his companions was the spread of the Greek culture throughout the area in which Paul would be traveling. Alexander the Great (356–323 B.C.), who toward the end of his life was not averse to being looked upon as a god himself, was really nothing more than a pawn in the hand of the one true God, who was readying all things for the fullness of time. Within the space of just a few years, 336–331 B.C., Alexander, a Macedonian, built an empire by military might that stretched from Illyria to India, from the Black Sea to Egypt. Wherever he went, he brought with him the Greek culture—its art, its poetry, its literature, its philosophy, and, especially, its language.

Wherever a person traveled in Alexander's empire, the Greek language was understood and spoken, especially in the major cities. All of God's plans for Paul had to do with words, with a spoken, and later also written, message. We see the blessed hand of

God at work through Alexander's Hellenization of the world, which made it possible for Paul to be understood no matter where he traveled. Compare the situation then with what prevails now in many parts of the world. Some of the nations in Africa have many different languages within just one country so that a missionary who is understood in one community may not be understood in another not many miles away.

Not only was it a blessing of God that the majority of people among whom Paul worked could understand the same language; it was also a special gift of God that this language was the Greek language, "the richest and most delicate the world has seen," as Conybeare and Howson put it.[7] Those who have had the privilege of learning the Greek language, and of using it in personal study of the Word and in preparation for preaching and teaching, can readily identify with what Conybeare and Howson say. To communicate with mankind, God saw fit to put his Word into words. To use the Greek language with all its subtleties and nuances as one of his primary means of communication is certainly again not mere happenstance. God wanted his message through Paul to be communicated to us as clearly and unambiguously as possible. So he used Alexander to make the beautiful Greek language the *lingua franca* of the area in which Paul would travel.

There were other less desirable features of Greek culture that Alexander brought with him, namely Greek philosophy and religion. The primary philosophies of the day were Epicureanism and Stoicism. Epicureanism, named for its founder, Epicurus (341–270 B.C.), held that pleasure was the chief goal of life. But because many pleasures are transient and leave painful aftereffects, Epicurus pointed to the pleasures of the mind as having the greatest value.

Later Epicureanism, however, tended to degenerate into a hedonistic quest for sensual pleasure, with an "eat, drink, and be merry, for tomorrow we die" approach to life. Such was a logical conclusion to this philosophy, for though the Epicureans didn't deny the existence of gods, they held that the gods remained aloof from what was going on in the world and that the soul dissipated at death. Paul showed that he understood well this philosophy and the hopelessness it generated when, writing to the Corinthians, he said, "If the dead are not raised, 'Let us eat and drink, for tomorrow we die'" (1 Corinthians 15:32).

The Stoics took their name from the place where the founder of that philosophy, Zeno (340–265 B.C.), did his teaching. He taught in the *Stoa,* the Painted Portico, in Athens, the same spot that once had been the meeting place of the poets. Unlike Epicurus, who was a deist, Zeno was a pantheist. He identified god with nature or with the reason or providence that guides and determines nature. He viewed history as a series of predetermined cycles, at the end of which the world will be destroyed by fire; but then it will be renewed to repeat another cycle with the same end, such a progression to go on forever.

He saw man as an absolutely helpless pawn in this preordained plan. The best that man can do is simply to "go with the flow," submit his will to the divine will of nature, join it rather than try to beat it. Epictetus, a spokesman for Stoicism, wrote: "Ask not that events should happen as you will, but let your will be that events should happen as they do, and you shall have peace."[8] Since everything is predetermined and nothing is changeable, one has to learn to accept things as they are with an inward detachment. This is the advice of Epictetus: "When you see a man shedding tears in sorrow for a child abroad or dead . . . do not hesitate to sympathize with him so far as words go, and if it so chance, even to groan with him; but take heed that you do not also groan in your inner being."[9]

Stoics also denied an afterlife or at best intimated that the soul merged with "god" at death. Paul, by the way, was most likely also well acquainted with the philosophy of Stoicism since Tarsus was the seat of an important Stoic school.

Epicureanism and Stoicism represent the two main ways by which people yet today try to come to terms with their earthly existence apart from Christ. Either, like the Epicureans, they determine to suck the last drop of juice out of life because that is all there is; or like the Stoics they resign themselves to drift along helplessly and hopelessly because no one can do anything about anything. Both ultimately are empty philosophies of despair. To those Greeks brought up on a diet of such "wisdom" came Paul with the "foolishness" of the gospel:

> It is written: "I will destroy the wisdom of the wise; the intelligence of the intelligent I will frustrate." Where is the wise man? Where is the scholar? Where is the philosopher of this age? Has not God made foolish the wisdom of the world? For since in the wisdom of God the world through its wisdom did not know him, God was pleased through the foolishness of what was preached to save those who believe. (1 Corinthians 1:19-21)

But even before Paul came preaching the gospel to turn people's hearts to the God who gives life and meaning and eternity, people were turning away from the hopeless note of the philosophies of the day. Sad to say, however, they were turning to an equally hopeless alternative: the mystery religions. Their appeal was that they offered what such philosophies as Stoicism and Epicureanism denied people: a guarantee of immortality. They often also offered to the initiate protection from the misfortunes and ills of everyday life. With their colorful pageantry and ecstatic rites they provided the emotional satisfaction of a "religious experience."

Some of the mystery religions, for example, the Eleusinian and Orphic Mysteries (with its Dionysian rites), had their origins in Greek mythology. Others originated in Egypt, for example, the rites of Isis and Osiris, and still others in the East, for example, Mithraism.

Although each of the mystery religions had its distinct features, they had certain characteristics in common. For one thing, they offered a secret knowledge of divine affairs not available to everyone, which Gnosticism would later pick up on and amplify. For another, they were all fertility cults, basing their activities on the cycles of the seasons, from death to life. As such their appeal was generally sensual and sexual. The worship, as is well known, was often accompanied by orgiastic behavior. The rites performed in the temples, both in respect to the objects of worship and the actions accompanying the worship, were filthy and degrading almost beyond description. Paul appears to be including this kind of worship when he exhorts the Ephesians:

> I tell you this, and insist on it in the Lord, that you must no longer live as the Gentiles do, in the futility of their thinking. They are darkened in their understanding and separated from the life of God because of the ignorance that is in them due to the

hardening of their hearts. Having lost all sensitivity, they have given themselves over to sensuality so as to indulge in every kind of impurity, with a continual lust for more.

Have nothing to do with the fruitless deeds of darkness, but rather expose them. For it is shameful even to mention what the disobedient do in secret (Ephesians 4:17-19; 5:11,12).

Some maintain that since these mystery religions were especially degrading to women, this helps to account for the fact that a considerable number of women were turning to the teaching of Judaism with its high moral tone. At any rate, Luke makes specific mention of women becoming converts to Christianity through the preaching of Paul in the synagogue. In Thessalonica, for example, we are told that "some of the Jews were persuaded and joined Paul and Silas, as did a large number of God-fearing Greeks and not a few prominent women" (Acts 17:4). In Berea, likewise, "many of the Jews believed, as did also a number of prominent Greek women and many Greek men" (Acts 17:12).

The world into which Paul moved with the gospel was also a world that gave much credence to the occult. Even educated people believed that an enemy could harass them by means of incantations. Plutarch spoke of rites that were instituted to propitiate and keep off evil demons, such as the devouring of raw flesh, mangling of bodies, fastings, beatings of the breast, obscene cries at the altars, and so on.[10] Roland Allen quotes a Dr. Bigg: "It is probably not too hard a thing to say that demon worship was the really operative religion of the vast mass of the people of the empire."[11]

Astrology, imported from Babylon, was accepted by many because of its claim to scientific accuracy. Those who leaned toward the Stoic philosophy found themselves attracted to astrology because it tended to reinforce the fatalistic attitude of the Stoics. Astrology was also seen as a unifying force in the Hellenization of the world; for no matter where people lived, no matter how far they were separated by geography or culture, all people had the same heavens above them. Astrology could thus serve as a one-world religion.

In short, the religious scene that Paul encountered in the Hellenistic world was not unlike what it is today. Stoicism and

Epicureanism are still prevalent philosophies, though the names may have changed. Demon worship, astrology, divination, witchcraft, magic, Gnostic systems—none of this is unheard of today. New Age religion is hardly new.[12]

It is helpful to note that Paul did not back away from confronting the false philosophies and religions of his day. It is also helpful to note *how* he did this. He did not simply attack them; rather, he vigorously set before his hearers the self-authenticating, liberating truth of the gospel. He did not ignore the philosophies of the Greeks. He became acquainted with them and then met them head-on with a superior weapon. The "wisdom" of Greek philosophy turned out to be no match for the "foolishness" of Paul's preaching.

Nor did Paul, as he went out into the world, simply ignore the magic and astrology all around him. He didn't dismiss it as idle, harmless superstition that had nothing behind it. He recognized the powerful hand of Satan in the various practices of the occult, and he confronted Satan with the even more powerful Word of Christ.

In Philippi, Paul was harassed by the demon-possessed girl who had the power to predict the future. He knew that it was not the girl herself, but the evil spirit in the girl, who was the real problem. So he ordered the spirit, "In the name of Jesus Christ I command you to come out of her!" (Acts 16:18). It did, at that very moment. The Word prevailed.

Ephesus was a center of magic in Paul's time. Many earned their living from the practice of magical arts or the selling of artifacts connected with magic. Paul came with the Word of the Lord, which proved to be more powerful than the practitioners of the magical arts. Even some of the sorcerers themselves came to faith and as a fruit of faith burned their books of magic (Acts 19:13-20).

To the believers in Ephesus, this hub of demonic religious practices, Paul wrote:

> Be strong in the Lord and in his mighty power. Put on the full armor of God so that you can take your stand against the devil's schemes. For our struggle is not against flesh and blood, but against the rulers, against the authorities, against the powers of this dark world and against the spiritual forces of evil in the heavenly realms. Stand firm then, with the belt of truth buckled

around your waist, with the breastplate of righteousness in place, and with your feet fitted with the readiness that comes from the gospel of peace. In addition to all this, take up the shield of faith, with which you can extinguish all the flaming arrows of the evil one. Take the helmet of salvation and the sword of the Spirit, which is the word of God. (Ephesians 6:10-12,14-17)

From Paul we learn to avoid two extremes when dealing with the philosophies and various "-isms" of the day. The one extreme would be to ignore them, to pretend that they do not exist. The other would be to center our attention on them, to spend the majority of our time on the defensive, attacking them. The golden mean, which Paul followed, would be to familiarize ourselves with the major philosophic and religious tenets of the people among whom we are called to work and then to confront error by going on the offensive with the powerful Word of Jesus Christ, confident that it has the power to free people who are caught in Satan's web of false philosophy or false religion.

In a most marvelous way, God had prepared the world for the day when he sent out Paul with the gospel. There was the Jewish Diaspora, which provided Paul with a base of operations in community after community. There was the Hellenization of the world after the time of Alexander, which gave the world into which Paul would travel one basic language as well as empty philosophies and religions, leaving a void that only Christianity could fill. We want to look at one further aspect of God's preparation of the world for the spread of the gospel: the *Pax Romana*.

Pax Romana

Again, we see that it is hardly by accident that the ascendancy of the power of Rome happened precisely at the time God determined to send forth his Son and then to send forth the message about his Son's finished work to the world. Five emperors ruled during this time. With Octavian (27 B.C.–A.D. 14), who took the title Augustus, the Roman Empire began and with it the *Pax Romana* (Roman peace). He was followed by the capable administrator Tiberius (A.D. 14–37). After the short reign of Caligula (A.D. 37–41), who was assassinated, Claudius, another able administrator, became emperor (A.D. 41–54). And then came Nero (A.D. 54–68).

During this whole period of time, and thus throughout Paul's missionary career, war practically ceased. The whole Mediterranean world was under one government. Those who enjoyed Roman citizenship were in an especially advantageous situation wherever they traveled in the empire. There was a universal toleration of all religions, a condition that was to change at the time of Nero. Travel had never been so easy or so safe. The system of Roman roads throughout the empire was unrivaled until recent times. At considerable expense Rome constructed harbors and bridges. Already under Pompey it had succeeded in ridding the seas of the Cilician pirates who had made travel by sea a risky business.

Paul made good use of these advantages God provided at that particular time through the Romans. Much of his travel was on two main Roman roads, the *Via Sebaste*, which stretched all the way from the Euphrates through Galatia and Asia to Ephesus, and the *Via Egnatia*, which began at Byzantium and ran west to Philippi and Thessalonica and then across the Balkan peninsula to Dyrrhachium and its port Egnatia on the Adriatic coast. The travel that Paul did by sea is well known. His first journey began with a short voyage to the island of Cyprus and from there to Pamphylia. Every missionary journey thereafter included lengthy sea voyages, culminated by his final voyage to Rome.

The *Pax Romana* didn't guarantee absolute safety. In 2 Corinthians Paul speaks about being "in danger from bandits" (11:26). Overall, however, it was a time marked by free movement from place to place on land or sea. Harnack, for example, mentions a Phrygian merchant who made the journey from Phrygia to Rome 72 times in his life.[13]

Religious toleration, protection, ease of travel—these were some of the great strengths of the Roman rule, strengths that Paul put to good use. There were weaknesses too, notably Roman cruelty, as seen particularly in the spectacles of the amphitheaters. The amphitheaters were built for shows of gladiators. Very little opposition was voiced against them. Allen quotes Dr. Bigg: "[There are] but three passages in which heathen writers express anything like adequate condemnation" of this activity.[14] Pliny and Cicero defended them as "affording a splendid training for the eye, though perhaps not for the ear, in the endurance of pain and death, and as inspiring disdain of death and love of honorable wounds." Symmachus expressed anger that some Saxons committed suicide in their cells rather than kill one another in public at the show he had prepared in honor of his son's praetorship.

Such lack of feeling and cruelty carried over into other aspects of life: into the theater and into the government of the day. Conybeare and Howson make the judgment that "we need not hesitate to take it for granted that those who were sent from Rome to dispense justice . . . were more frequently like . . . Pilate and Felix, than Gallio and Sergius Paulus."[15]

What did this mean for the spread of the gospel? Conybeare and Howson go too far when, after describing the temper of the times as "essentially both cruel and profane," they state that "the human race was groaning for the better peace of a 'kingdom not of this world.'"[16] The evils of a society will not lead people to long for the gospel. But it is true that difficult times tend to make people more ready to listen to a message that promises something better, much as today an unbeliever who has just suffered the loss of all he has will tend to be more willing to listen to the Christian message than one who has just won a million dollars in the lottery. Even the negative aspects of the Roman rule, then, served a positive purpose. (An example would be slavery, which will be discussed later in another connection.) Paul came preaching in a world that quite clearly was far from ideal, a world that left much room for people's longings for something better. Paul's gospel filled that longing—and then some.

Three distinct blessings of God made the times right for the spread of the gospel: the Diaspora, the Greek culture, and the Roman peace. Paul took advantage of them all: the migration of Jews into the Mediterranean world, the synagogue, the Septuagint, the Greek language, the emptiness of Greek philosophy and religion, the privileges of Roman citizenship, and the relative ease of Roman transportation.

As we today consider the call to make disciples of all nations, it will do us well also to discern the times and take advantage of whatever opportunities the Lord sets before us, both here in the United States and abroad. As in Paul's day so today, both positive aspects, like modern methods of communication, and negative ones, like the breakdown of the family, can be allies of those whose goal is to evangelize in their communities.

Paul clearly understood his times and interpreted what was going on around him, in terms of what impact this might have on the spread of the gospel. We too will want to "read" our society, not simply to marvel at its advancement and deplore its disintegration in so many areas but in order to develop mission strategies that will maximize every opportunity to turn loose the one power that saves—the gospel of Jesus Christ.

Study Questions

1. Read the following passages. After you have read them, discuss what Paul might have said if he had heard that future generations would be studying the story of his life.

   • Romans 15:17,18 *focus more on God's*
   actions + grace than
   • 1 Corinthians 15:9 *my life*
   • 1 Corinthians 15:10

   • 1 Timothy 1:13,14

2. In spite of what Paul might have said, why are we making a study of his life? *to see how God uses his grace to put people to do his work*

3. Paul was an apostle, a fact he had to repeat often since many thought he did not have the credentials of the other apostles. He had not personally accompanied Jesus during his ministry. How do the following verses and key words tell us that Paul did possess the credentials of the other apostles?

   • 1 Corinthians 2:10-13 (Authority) *God gave him the words to speak*
   • 1 Corinthians 9:1 (Eyewitness) *he has seen God + what God has done through himself*
   • 2 Corinthians 12:12 (Special powers) *he did miracles - drove out demons*
   • Galatians 1:1 (Commission) *Sent by God*

4. The Lord shaped events so that his Word could be spread throughout the world. What was the Diaspora? How did it help Paul do his missionary work? How did Paul use Jewish synagogues in his outreach? *Diaspora spread Jews who had a knowledge of God's Word around. Paul preached the Word to those who gathered.*

5. Have you ever been part of a nucleus of a new congregation? Share your experiences. *no*

6. How was the spread of the Word made easier because Jews had migrated to Egypt? (Hint: What translation of the Bible was made in Egypt that provided the foundation for Paul's mission work, especially to the Gentiles?) *the Septuagint was written*

7. Julius Caesar gave Jews throughout the world the right to practice their religion. How did this help Paul spread God's Word? *he was free from gov't persecution*

8. The English language today is an international language. To an even greater degree, Greek was the international language in Paul's world. How did this help the spread of the gospel? *no language barriers in expressing saving grace*

9. How does the fact that English is an international language today help our world missionaries spread the gospel? *we won't have God's message lost in translation*

10. Reread 1 Corinthians 1:19-21. What was the "wisdom" that the Greeks considered so valuable? (Hint: Think of the two main philosophies of that day.) What was Paul's (and our) answer to the world's wisdom? *— Epicureanism + Stoicism — Gospel (Christ crucified)*

11. Paul's world was filled with occult religions and practitioners. How did Paul (and how should we) combat these forces of evil? *was familiar + trusted God's Word*

12. What is meant by the *Pax Romana?* How did the Lord use this to help the spread of his Word? Consider the following topics:

    • warfare *no wars to worry about*

    • roads *easier to travel, safe from robbers*

    • sea travel *safe from pirates*

13. Agree or disagree: The evils of society will lead people to long for the gospel. *it will make them more receptive*

14. Although people by nature do not yearn for God's grace and forgiveness, why are these blessings, which we have to share, the ultimate answer to everyone's needs?
    they show that earthly matters don't matter, we have eternal life in heaven

*Part Two*_____

Paul's Early Years

IN THE FIRST PART OF THIS STUDY, we talked about the marvelous way
in which the Lord prepared the *world* for Paul's mission endeavors.
In this part our emphasis will be on the way the Lord prepared *Paul*
for going out into the world with the gospel. The main facts are
quite well known to us. From childhood we have thrilled to hear
the account of the conversion of the Christ-hating Saul, to hear
how God turned his life around, to hear how this persecutor of
Jesus became Jesus' most ardent supporter. We intend in Part 2 to
look in somewhat more detail at how the Lord accomplished this
and prepared Saul for a lifetime of missionary activity. Then we will
make some applications to preparation for mission work today.

Preconversion days

Paul was born into a world dominated by Greek culture and
ruled by Roman might, a world that had seen much movement of
peoples, particularly the Jews, who now conservatively numbered
six times as many living outside of Palestine as inside it. Paul was
a part of all of this. He was a Jew. He had a good understanding of

the Greek culture. He was a Roman citizen. Again, it is hardly by accident that the Lord called this particular man to be his "chosen instrument to carry my name before the Gentiles and their kings and before the people of Israel" (Acts 9:15).

A Greek

Three times the book of Acts refers to the fact that Paul was from Tarsus. The Lord identifies the man whom Ananias is to visit in Damascus as "a man from Tarsus named Saul" (Acts 9:11). During his final visit to Jerusalem, when his life is endangered by an out-of-control mob, Paul identifies himself to his protector, Claudius Lysias, the commander of the Roman troops housed in the fortress of Antonia adjacent to the temple: "I am a Jew, from Tarsus in Cilicia, a citizen of no ordinary city" (Acts 21:39). Then, when the crowd is quieted down, Paul opens his address to it with similar words: "I am a Jew, born in Tarsus of Cilicia" (Acts 22:3).

Tarsus, Paul says, is "no *ordinary* city" (in Greek, "unmarked"; figuratively, "obscure, insignificant"). He makes an effective use of a litotes here to emphasize the fact that Tarsus was far from an ordinary city, that it was in fact a significant, important metropolis. Tarsus was located in Cilicia, a border province, and thus of some importance to the Romans, especially since Cilicia was home to the rugged Taurus Mountains and the narrow pass through these mountains, the Cilician Gates. Control of that pass was vital to Roman security. The Romans established some control in Cilicia by around 100 B.C. and then solidified that control in 67 B.C. at the time of Pompey's successful military campaign against the Cilician pirates. The Roman statesman and philosopher Cicero served as proconsul there from 51–50 B.C.

Cilicia was divided into two parts, the mostly mountainous Western (or Rough) Cilicia and Eastern (or Level) Cilicia, which from 25 B.C. on was united administratively with Syria to the east and south. It is likely Eastern Cilicia to which Paul is referring in Galatians when he says that some time subsequent to his conversion he went to Syria and Cilicia (Galatians 1:21).

Tarsus was in Eastern Cilicia on the Cydnus River, about 10 miles from its mouth and about 30 miles from the Taurus Mountains and the Cilician Gates. At the time of Paul, it was the capital of the province of Cilicia; but it also held the status of a free city, exempted by Augustus from imperial taxation.

The city was a center of commerce. The Tarsians had built a road through the Cilician Gates, which helped to make the city, already a seaport, also a hub of an important land trade route, situated as it was right between the East and the West. It was a large city. Some suggest that the population at its height may have numbered close to 500,000. It was prosperous. Situated on a fertile plain, it became well known for its linen that was woven from flax grown in the plain and also for cilicium, woven from goat's hair, which made coverings that gave protection against cold and moisture. Paul undoubtedly would have learned how to work with cilicium.

Of considerable significance for the work that the Lord had planned for Paul is the fact that Tarsus was a center of Greek culture. E. M. Blaiklock writes:

> It became the Athens of the eastern Mediterranean, the ancient equivalent of a university city, the resort of men of learning, the home town of Athenodorus (74 B.C.–A.D. 7), the respected teacher of Augustus himself, the seat of a school of Stoic philosophers, a place of learning and disputation, the very climate in which a brilliant mind might grow up in the midst of stimulus and challenge and learn to think and to contend.[17]

The geographer Strabo (first century?) describes the people of Tarsus as avid in the pursuit of culture—of philosophy and the liberal arts. F. F. Bruce remarks that, in this respect at least, the citizens of Tarsus "surpassed even Athens and Alexandria, whose schools were frequented more by visitors than by their own citizens."[18]

Born in Tarsus and raised there, at least for a time, Paul had the opportunity to become acquainted with Greek culture. In his defense before the people in Jerusalem, Paul says, according to the NIV translation, "I am a Jew, born in Tarsus of Cilicia, but brought up in this city. Under Gamaliel I was thoroughly trained in the law" (Acts 22:3). This translation would seem to indicate that from a very early age Paul's home was Jerusalem. The Greek, however, can also be translated, "I am a Jew, born in Tarsus of Cilicia, but brought up in this city at the feet of Gamaliel, thoroughly trained in the law." This translation seems preferable. Paul, then, would have been sent away from home sometime in his teens to complete his education. The Greek verb, translated in the NIV in its participial form as "brought up," in Greek writings often has the predominant idea of forming the mind, something that Gamaliel, of course, would have sought to do.

Greek may well have been Paul's native tongue. The writings of the Greek poets and philosophers were not unknown to him. In Athens he quotes the Cilician poet Aratus (around 300 B.C.): "We are his offspring," as well as the Cretan poet Epimenides (around 600 B.C.): "In him we live and move and have our being" (Acts 17:28). He quotes Epimenides again when writing to Titus: "Cretans are always liars, evil brutes, lazy gluttons" (Titus 1:12). A line from a comedy by another Greek poet, Menander, is found in Paul's well-known resurrection chapter: "Bad company corrupts good character" (1 Corinthians 15:33).

From his upbringing in Tarsus, Paul would also have become acquainted with one of the lower elements of Greek culture: its gross pagan worship. The chief god of Tarsus was Baal Tars. A secondary deity was Sandan, the worship of whom figured heavily in fertility rites climaxed annually by a funeral observance representing the death of this god of vegetation. This was followed by a celebration of his resurrection, a resurrection celebrated with all kinds of immoral sexual behavior.[19]

Paul, then, from his formative years in Tarsus would have seen firsthand some of the best and worst of Greek culture. From what he had learned in his early years, he was able to speak to the Greeks as a Greek.

A Roman

Likewise he could speak to the Romans as a Roman. Luke records in Acts the following dialogue between Paul and the Roman commander Claudius Lysias (Acts 22:27,28):

> Claudius Lysias: "Tell me, are you a Roman citizen?"
> Paul: "Yes, I am."
> Claudius Lysias: "I had to pay a big price for my citizenship."
> Paul: "But I was born a citizen."

This indicates that Paul's father was a Roman citizen. It could have gone back even further than that, of course. Just how citizenship was conferred on Paul's family is not stated. Originally Roman citizenship was granted only to freeborn natives of the city of Rome, but by this time the rights of citizenship had been extended far beyond that group. At times individuals or groups who had rendered some special service to help the Roman cause were awarded with Roman citizenship. Once conferred, citizenship was transmitted by birth. It is possible that already at the time of Pompey many of the inhabitants of Tarsus had been granted Roman citizenship. Tarsus tended to receive favored treatment because it was, in effect, the guardian of the Cilician Gates, which were so vital to the defense of the Empire.

At any rate, Paul enjoyed the privilege of Roman citizenship, a privilege that he did not fail to use as the situation warranted. There were several such occasions. In Philippi, Paul and Silas were beaten. The next day the magistrate ordered them to be released. Paul spoke up on behalf of himself and Silas: "They beat us publicly without a trial, even though we are Roman citizens, and threw us into prison. And now do they want to get rid of us quietly? No! Let them come themselves and escort us out" (Acts 16:37). With these words Paul demonstrated that he knew well the protections afforded by Roman citizenship. Every Roman citizen was entitled to a fair public trial if he was accused of any crime. He was exempted from certain ignominious forms of punishment, and he was protected against summary execution.

Paul took advantage of these same rights later in Jerusalem, following his third missionary journey. Claudius Lysias had given the command for Paul to be flogged. The soldiers were stretching out his body and were about to begin the flogging when Paul brought this activity to a halt by asking, "Is it legal for you to flog a Roman citizen who hasn't even been found guilty?" (Acts 22:25). Some two years later, when Festus succeeded Felix as governor of Judea, Paul again availed himself of the privilege of Roman citizenship. Festus wanted to bring him up to Jerusalem from Caesarea, where he had been held prisoner for the past two years. Convinced that he could not receive a fair trial in Jerusalem, Paul told Festus, "I appeal to Caesar" (Acts 25:11). To Rome he went, then, where even though he was under arrest for two whole years, as a Roman citizen speaking to Roman citizens, "boldly and without hindrance he preached the kingdom of God and taught about the Lord Jesus Christ" (Acts 28:31).

A Jew

And Paul could also speak to the Jews as a Jew. He describes himself in Philippians as "circumcised on the eighth day, of the people of Israel, of the tribe of Benjamin, a Hebrew of Hebrews; in regard to the law, a Pharisee" (Philippians 3:5). The tribe of Benjamin was one of the two that made up the Southern Kingdom. Though Benjamin was drawn into the larger Judah, at least some Benjamites didn't allow their ancestry to be obliterated. Nehemiah mentions certain descendants of Benjamin who settled in Jerusalem and in other communities when they returned from captivity (Nehemiah 11:7-9,31-36). The tribe of Benjamin's most illustrious member up until the time of Paul was King Saul. Was the New Testament Saul/Paul so named because of this ancestor? We might note here, by the way, that the name Paul probably was not given later when he started his missionary journeys. It was more likely one of his given names as a Roman citizen, a name that Luke uses exclusively of him, beginning with Paul's work on the island of Cyprus on his first missionary journey and on to the end of the book of Acts (Acts 13:9).[20]

We are not told in the Scriptures the circumstances or the time of the migration of Paul's family to Tarsus. They could possibly have been there for several generations. We know, for example, that Antiochus IV (175–164 B.C.) transplanted a group of Jewish families there to strengthen his hold on Asia Minor. Jerome (around A.D. 400), however, who lived in Bethlehem for a time, states that Paul's parents fled to Tarsus from Gischala in Galilee during the time of the Roman takeover of Palestine in the first century B.C.

At any rate, the family, though it lived in a gentile culture, did not lose its Jewish heritage. Paul calls himself "a Hebrew of Hebrews," likely in contrast to calling himself a Hellenistic Jew. His father and apparently his grandfather before him were Pharisees, for he describes himself as "a Pharisee, the son of a Pharisee" (Acts 23:6). (The NIV translates "the son of a Pharisee," but in the Greek

Pharisee is in the plural.) In his childhood, then, even before his training under Gamaliel, Paul would certainly have become very familiar with the tenets of Judaism. A Jewish boy would begin his study of the Scriptures at age 5 and the study of the legal traditions of the Jews at age 10.

From early on, Paul would have learned a trade. Jewish education sought to produce a man who could both think and do. A Jewish rabbinical saying went this way: "Whosoever doth not teach his son work, teacheth him to rob." Gamaliel II is quoted as saying: "Excellent is Torah study together with worldly business, for all Torah without work must fail at length, and occasion iniquity."[21]

This part of his upbringing also stood him in good stead, enabling him to support himself through tent making, so no one could accuse him of evangelizing for financial gain. In his farewell to the Ephesian elders, he said, "These hands of mine have supplied my own needs and the needs of my companions" (Acts 20:34). To the Corinthians he writes, "We work hard with our own hands" (1 Corinthians 4:12). Even though he had the right to get his living from the gospel, he chose not to use that right (1 Corinthians 9:6-15). "We worked night and day in order not to be a burden to anyone," he reminds the Thessalonians (1 Thessalonians 2:9). He probably preached and taught during the day and did his tent making at night.

Like his father and grandfather, Paul became a Pharisee, "the strictest sect of our religion," as he himself put it (Acts 26:5). The Pharisees, a name that probably means "separated ones," denoting their policy of strict separation from anything that might smack of moral or ceremonial impurity, are mentioned by Josephus as being in existence already by about 150 B.C.[22] They probably rose from the ranks of the Hasidim, a group of Jews who banded themselves together following the return from exile to encourage one another in the study and practice of the Law. Many of them joined up with the Hasmoneans against the Seleucids who tried to force Hellenization upon the Jews. According to Josephus the Pharisees numbered about six thousand.[23]

It is likely that Paul was in his early teens when he was sent to Jerusalem to begin his training under Gamaliel, since it was after their bar mitzvah that the more promising boys were directed into the rabbinic schools. He may have lived in the home of his sister. (Acts 23:16 mentions "the son of Paul's sister," who alerted Paul to a plot against his life when he was in custody in Rome.)

Gamaliel I was one of the greatest rabbis of the first century. It was this Gamaliel, "who was honored by all the people," whose moderate wait-and-see counsel in regard to the followers of Jesus was adopted by the Sanhedrin. "If their purpose or activity is of human origin, it will fail," he said. "But if it is from God, you will not be able to stop these men; you will only find yourselves fighting against God" (Acts 5:34,38,39).

In this counsel Gamaliel was apparently not reflecting the stringent and conservative school of Shammai but rather the spirit of the more humanitarian and liberal school of Hillel, of which he was a part. A later tradition, in fact, says that Gamaliel was Hillel's grandson. Gamaliel's most well-known student, Saul of Tarsus, obviously did not follow his counsel.

But Saul did follow the law as taught by the Pharisees. He tells the Galatians: "I was advancing in Judaism beyond many Jews of my own age and was extremely zealous for the traditions of my fathers" (Galatians 1:14). "As for legalistic righteousness," he tells the Philippians, righteousness that comes in connection with the law, he was "faultless" (Philippians 3:6). In his defense before Agrippa, he simply said, "I lived as a Pharisee," a fact, he says, to which anyone who knew him either in Tarsus or Jerusalem could certainly testify (Acts 26:5).

He understood what it meant to be a Jew and thus could meet them on their own turf. He could look back on his own life as evidence when he wrote about the Jews: "I can testify about them that they are zealous for God, but their zeal is not based on knowledge. . . . They did not know the righteousness that comes from God and sought to establish their own" (Romans 10:2,3). Because of that misguided zeal, Paul says of the Jews, "I have great sorrow and unceasing anguish in my heart" (Romans 9:2), a heart that longed to evangelize these people with whom he had so much in common.

A persecutor

It took a mighty miracle of God, however, to put that kind of knowledge and feeling into Paul's heart. When we first meet Paul in the Scriptures, he is zealously, though mistakenly, upholding the traditions of his fathers. At the stoning of Stephen, "I stood there," he recalls some 25 years later, "giving my approval and guarding the clothes of those who were killing him" (Acts 22:20). Paul recognized, as clearly as Stephen did on the other side, the incompatibility between Judaism as he had been taught and Christianity. It had to be one or the other. We see here the same refusal to compromise that marked Paul's later life as an apostle. God rechannels people's strengths into his service.

For a few years, though, it was anything but *God's* service in which Paul was involved. "You have heard of my previous way of life in Judaism," he told the Galatians, "how intensely I persecuted the church of God and tried to destroy it" (Galatians 1:13). "I was once a blasphemer and a persecutor and a violent man," he reminded Timothy (1 Timothy 1:13). In his defense before Agrippa, Paul confessed:

> I . . . was convinced that I ought to do all that was possible to oppose the name of Jesus of Nazareth. And that is just what I did in Jerusalem. On the authority of the chief priests I put many of the saints in prison, and when they were put to death, I cast my vote against them. Many a time I went from one synagogue to another to have them punished, and I tried to force them to blaspheme. In my obsession against them, I even went to foreign cities to persecute them. (Acts 26:9-11)

To the Jews in Jerusalem, he said:

> I persecuted the followers of this Way to their death, arresting both men and women and throwing them into prison, as also the high priest and all the Council can testify. I even obtained letters from them to their brothers in Damascus, and went there to bring these people as prisoners to Jerusalem to be punished. (Acts 22:4,5)

Conversion and post-conversion days

It is this man whom the Lord Jesus confronted on the Damascus road. The account, recorded in Acts 9:3-9, is familiar, as are Paul's autobiographical reminiscences of that day. Two times Paul speaks in some detail about his conversion, first to the crowd of Jews in Jerusalem (Acts 22:6-16) and then in even more detail when he

stands before King Agrippa in Caesarea (Acts 26:12-18). Our famil-
iarity with this account, however, should not be allowed to dimin-
ish in our minds the magnitude of what transpired. For Paul it was
a matter of never-ceasing amazement. Writing to Timothy some 30
years later, Paul said:

> Here is a trustworthy saying that deserves full acceptance: Christ
> Jesus came into the world to save sinners—of whom I am the
> worst. But for that very reason I was shown mercy so that in me,
> the worst of sinners, Christ Jesus might display his unlimited
> patience as an example for those who would believe on him and
> receive eternal life. (1 Timothy 1:15,16)

The thought of this overwhelming mercy of God toward him
simply overwhelms Paul and leads him to break out in the beautiful doxology, "Now to the King eternal, immortal, invisible,
the only God, be honor and glory for ever and ever. Amen"
(1 Timothy 1:17).

His life was completely turned around from that day forward.
He tells the Philippians:

> Whatever was to my profit I now consider loss for the sake of
> Christ. What is more, I consider everything a loss compared to
> the surpassing greatness of knowing Christ Jesus my Lord, for
> whose sake I have lost all things. I consider them rubbish, that I
> may gain Christ and be found in him, not having a righteousness
> of my own that comes from the law, but that which is through
> faith in Christ—the righteousness that comes from God and is by
> faith. I want to know Christ and the power of his resurrection
> and the fellowship of sharing in his sufferings, becoming like
> him in his death, and so, somehow, to attain to the resurrection
> from the dead. (Philippians 3:7-11)

He wanted to know Christ. And he wanted to share Christ: "I
am compelled to preach. Woe to me if I do not preach the
gospel!" (1 Corinthians 9:16). That, of course, is exactly what the
Lord had in mind for Paul. Ananias relayed to Paul the Lord's call
to service: "The God of our fathers has chosen you to know his
will and to see the Righteous One and to hear words from his
mouth. You will be his witness to all men of what you have seen
and heard" (Acts 22:14,15).

Three years after his conversion, Paul went up to Jerusalem (Galatians 1:18). While he was praying in the temple he fell into a trance, during which the Lord repeated to Paul personally the call he had conveyed to him through Ananias. "Go," the Lord told him. "I will send you far away to the Gentiles" (Acts 22:21).

These two commissions are possibly combined and summarized by Paul in Acts chapter 26 when he tells Agrippa that the Lord told him:

> I have appeared to you to appoint you as a servant and as a witness of what you have seen of me and what I will show you. I will rescue you from your own people and from the Gentiles. I am sending you to them to open their eyes and turn them from darkness to light, and from the power of Satan to God, so that they may receive forgiveness of sins and a place among those who are sanctified by faith in me. (Acts 26:16-18)

With utmost confidence Paul can describe himself as "Paul, an apostle—sent not from men nor by man, but by Jesus Christ and God the Father, who raised him from the dead" (Galatians 1:1).

It was to be some time, however, before Paul would be deemed ready to carry out what we today call his three missionary journeys. The Lord took about 15 years following Paul's conversion, in fact, to prepare him for going out into the world with the gospel. Acts chapters 9,11,12,22, and 26; 2 Corinthians 11:29-33; and the first, and perhaps second, chapter of Galatians furnish us with the material that fleshes out these years. They may be reconstructed as follows:

1. Conversion and commissioning, around A.D. *32 (Acts 9:1-19)*

Paul heads for Damascus, about 150 miles northeast of Jerusalem, to find followers of "the Way" (Acts 9:2) whom he might bring back bound to Jerusalem. Josephus tells us that Julius Caesar, in 47 B.C., had granted the right of extradition to the high priest.[24] Damascus, with its large concentration of Jews, between 10,000 and 18,000,[25] seemed to be a good place to go for this purpose.

2. Preaching in Damascus (Acts 9:19b-22)

We are told that following his conversion "Saul spent several days with the disciples in Damascus. *At once* he began to preach in the synagogues that Jesus is the Son of God" (Acts 9:19b,20, ital-ics added).

3. *To Arabia (Galatians 1:15-17)*

When one compares Galatians 1:15-17 with Acts 9:19-25, it is difficult to tell which came first, Paul's preaching in Damascus or his trip to Arabia. This is especially true when one looks at the NIV. In the Galatians account, Paul says that after his conversion and call he "went *immediately* [same word as Acts 9:20] into Arabia and later returned to Damascus" (Galatians 1:17). There appears, then, to be a conflict. Did Paul immediately preach in Damascus, or did he immediately go to Arabia? In the Greek of the Galatians passage, the word *immediately*, however, comes much earlier in the sentence. The point Paul is making centers on what he *did not* immediately do, not on what he *did* immediately do. He did not immediately consult any man, nor did he immediately go up to Jerusalem to get human authorization for his work. What he did do was go into Arabia. This doesn't preclude his doing something else prior to this as long as it had nothing to do with gaining per-mission from some human being to do what Christ himself had commissioned him to do.

We are assuming in this chronology, then, that the newly con-verted Paul immediately began to speak about Jesus in the syna-gogues of Damascus, but that shortly thereafter he went away to Arabia, after which he returned to Damascus to continue preach-ing until forced to leave. His trip to Arabia, then, would fit between verses 22 and 23 of Acts chapter 9.

Arabia, the kingdom of the Nabateans, was ruled by Aretas IV (9 B.C.–A.D. 40) during this time. Normally its territory was much farther south, but at times it reached as far north as Damascus. Damascus, in fact, may have been under the control of Aretas at this time (see 2 Corinthians 11:32). No Damascene coins from A.D. 34–62 bearing the image of the Roman emperor have been found, which "may indicate that the Romans recognized a Nabatean area of influence in the city."[26] Some, however, maintain that the gover-nor mentioned in 2 Corinthians chapter 11 didn't rule Damascus but was rather Aretas' representative to the Arabs living under Roman rule in Damascus.

We can only speculate on what Paul did during the time he spent in Arabia. The fact that Luke, who is deeply interested in recording the missionary activity of Paul, is completely silent about this trip, coupled with the context of Galatians (Paul doesn't mention any preaching until the end of the chapter) leads one to conclude that Paul did not spend his time in Arabia evangelizing but being prepared to evangelize. It would thus have been a time to meditate, to study, and perhaps to receive further revelations from the risen Lord. See, for example, 1 Corinthians 11:23: "I received from the Lord what I also passed on to you: The Lord Jesus, on the night he was betrayed, . . . "

4. *Return to Damascus (Acts 9:23-25; 2 Corinthians 11:32,33)*

His stay the second time in Damascus was cut short by the combined efforts of some Jews and the governor of King Aretas to arrest and kill him, an effort foiled by Paul's friends, who lowered him in a basket through an opening in the wall.

5. *First trip to Jerusalem, around* A.D. *35 (Acts 9:26-29; Galatians 1:18-20)*

Paul tells us that after three years he went up to Jerusalem. The three years would most logically be dated from his conversion. We don't know how much of the three years he spent in Damascus and how much in Arabia. We do know that at the end of this time period, he made a brief 15-day visit to Jerusalem. The only leaders of the church with whom he had a chance to visit were Peter and James, the Lord's brother; but he also spent some time moving about freely in Jerusalem, "speaking boldly in the name of the Lord" (Acts 9:28), especially to the Grecian Jews. But when these former allies turned on him and tried to kill him, his new Christian friends escorted him to Caesarea and sent him off to Tarsus.

6. *To Syria and Cilicia, around* A.D. *35–44 (Acts 9:30; Galatians 1:21)*

This is a silent time in the book of Acts, but it hardly appears to be a silent time in Paul's life. The united province of Syria-Cilicia was Paul's home country. He spent some ten years in this area, with Tarsus likely as his home base. From Galatians and Acts we receive a few clues as to Paul's activities during these ten years. The churches of Judea, where Paul was personally unknown, were hearing the report after Paul was sent to Syria and Cilicia: "The man who formerly persecuted us is now preaching the faith he once tried to destroy" (Galatians 1:23).

We have a few other clues as to Paul's activity during this time. There was the letter sent out following the Jerusalem Council. It was addressed "To the Gentile believers in Antioch, Syria and Cilicia" (Acts 15:23). A second clue: At the beginning of his second missionary journey, Paul "went through Syria and Cilicia, strengthening the churches" (Acts 15:41). Both of these passages assume the existence of churches in Syria and Cilicia, churches that were not founded during Paul's first journey and therefore must have been there even before that.

We are arguing from relative silence, of course, to maintain that Paul was responsible for the existence of many of these churches; but the Galatians passage cited in the previous paragraph, together with these passages from Acts chapter 15, do lend credence to the assumption that Paul did much evangelizing of a perhaps more spontaneous nature prior to what we today call his first missionary journey. It is also entirely possible that some of the suffering for the gospel that Paul mentions in 2 Corinthians 11:23-29, much of which is difficult to fit into the framework of the three missionary journeys, occurred during these approximately ten years.

7. *To Antioch of Syria, around* A.D. *45 (Acts 11:19-26)*

Situated on the Orontes River about 18 miles from the Mediterranean, Antioch was the provincial capital of Syria-Cilicia and the third largest city in the Roman Empire, after Rome and Alexandria. Located right on the dividing line between the Graeco-Roman world and the Orient, it was a center of commerce and a melting pot of Western and Eastern culture. Greek and Roman traditions mingled with Semitic, Arabic, and Persian influences.

Jews formed a part of Antioch's population from its founding in 350 B.C. Proselytes to Judaism were also abundant at the beginning of the Christian era.[27] The Nicolas mentioned in Acts 6:5 was one such convert.

Christianity came quite early to Antioch. Following Stephen's martyrdom, Jewish believers who were forced out of Jerusalem brought the message to Phoenicia, to the island of Cyprus, and to Antioch. At first they evangelized only their fellow Jews, but in time some of the Jews who were natives of Cyprus and Cyrene brought the gospel also to the Gentiles in Antioch. The account of the evangelization of Antioch may have been of special interest to Luke. (The anti-Marcionite prologue to the gospel of Luke [late second century] states that Luke was born in Antioch. Eusebius and Jerome, at a later date, say the same thing.)

Barnabas, a native of Cyprus (Acts 4:36), was sent from Jerusalem to give guidance and encouragement to the church at Antioch, a task for which he was well suited. Barnabas, which means "Son of Encouragement," was evidently a nickname with which the early church tagged this Levite named Joseph (Acts 4:36). Earlier he had encouraged the church in Jerusalem to receive Paul (Acts 9:27). Later he would encourage John Mark when Paul was ready to give up on him (Acts 15:37-39).

As the work in Antioch grew, Barnabas felt the need for assistance. He knew Paul, of course, and perhaps had heard of his evangelizing work in Syria and Cilicia. At any rate, he traveled to Tarsus, found Paul, and brought him back to Antioch. There, for one whole year, Barnabas and Paul taught the church, a church that was willing to part with its pastors in the interest of spreading the gospel even farther than Antioch.

8. *To Jerusalem for the famine visit, around* A.D. *46*
   (Acts 11:27-30; 12:25)

Before we explore some applications to our present day, we should look briefly at one other incident prior to Paul's first missionary journey, the famine visit to Jerusalem. This visit was significant for two reasons: First, it helps with dating the events in Paul's life since it refers to an incident also mentioned by historians of that day. Second, it illustrates one of the fruits of gospel preaching: It produces love for the brethren.

According to Agabus, a man with the spiritual gift of prophecy, a severe famine would spread over the entire Roman Empire. Luke, exhibiting his interest in historical precision, tells us that this famine occurred during the reign of Claudius (A.D. 41–54). Early historians (Suetonius, Tacitus, Eusebius) speak of a series of severe droughts during the time Claudius ruled.

Josephus tells us about one such famine in Palestine during the procuratorships of Cuspius Fadus (around A.D. 44–46) and his successor Tiberius Julius Alexander (around A.D. 46–48). A convert to Judaism, Helena, queen mother of Adiabene, east of the Tigris, and her son, King Izates, provided food and money for the famine stricken in Jerusalem at this time.[28] Helena, Josephus says, actually traveled to Jerusalem as a pilgrim with these gifts, which could well have been about the same time that Barnabas and Paul went up to Jerusalem with the offering from the saints in Antioch. In addition to this, papyri found in Egypt speak of the high price of grain in Egypt at this time, possibly evidence of a famine-caused shortage.[29] Dating the famine visit to Jerusalem at around A.D. 46 appears, then, to be fairly accurate.

The death of Herod Agrippa I is also mentioned in this context (Acts 12:23). His death occurred in A.D. 44, possibly about the same time that Agabus prophesied the coming of the famine. That Luke doesn't necessarily place the death of Herod and the famine visit of Barnabas and Paul at precisely the same time can be seen from the opening words of Acts chapter 12, "It was *about* this time that King Herod arrested some who belonged to the church." The various historical sources cited lead us to opt for a famine visit date a few years after Herod's death.

The concrete way by which the Christians of Antioch demonstrated their love to their brothers and sisters in Jerusalem would be repeated later on an even grander scale when the churches of Asia, Macedonia, and Achaia joined hands in a generous outpouring of aid to their fellow believers in Jerusalem (see 2 Corinthians 8,9).

This action of the believers in Antioch, and later in the other places Paul preached, serves as a good reminder to us that, though we properly separate justification and sanctification, practically speaking, the one will not exist apart from the other. Faith expresses itself through love, the first fruit of the Spirit (Galatians 5:6,22).

We can learn some valuable lessons about preparation for the ministry from the way the Lord prepared Paul.

We note, first of all, the need for a changed heart. "This is the one I esteem," the Lord says through his prophet Isaiah, "he who is humble and contrite in spirit, and trembles at my word" (Isaiah 66:2). That was the Lord's key step in preparing Paul. Everything else was preliminary. His upbringing in the tenets of Judaism, his fine grasp of Greek culture, his Roman citizenship, his zeal, his leadership abilities—all this was supportive but not foundational. We have seen how Paul, time and again, traced it all back—his whole mission career—to the day of his conversion when he personally tasted the grace of God, which he then felt compelled to give to others (1 Corinthians 9:16).

In our congregational life also, the best way to instill a missionary zeal is not to preach missions as a "must do" but to preach Christ as a "has done." Let his "It is finished!" and the angels' "He is risen!" resound in a positive, joyful manner from pulpit and lectern. Let that message continue to touch and change hearts. Let it create and build up faith, and a result will be, as it was with Paul, zeal on the part of our people to give away to others what God has so graciously given to them.

Second, as we look back upon the way the Lord prepared Paul for the ministry, *we see the value of a broad-based rather than a narrow-focused education.* In addition to the primary requisite of a changed heart, we note that Paul went out into the mission field well equipped in two different areas. From his upbringing at home and from the time spent in formal training at the feet of Gamaliel, it is clear that Paul was very much at home with the Scriptures. His sermons and other discourses in Acts and his epistles abound in quotations and allusions to the Old Testament. With his knowledge of the Scriptures, it was not difficult for him to do what he did in the synagogue at Thessalonica, for example, where, we are told, "on three Sabbath days he reasoned with them from the Scriptures, explaining and proving that the Christ had to suffer and rise from the dead" (Acts 17:2,3).

Paul was also well prepared in that he knew the society in which he would be working. He knew the religions; he knew the philosophies. He knew the weaknesses; he knew the glaring deficiencies. To this world he knew, Paul applied the Word he knew. These, to a large degree, were his qualifications: his solid grounding in the Scriptures and his considerable knowledge of his times. He was comfortable in both worlds and knew how to bring the one to the other.

There is always a certain tension in a seminary's curriculum. What should be the ratio of so-called theoretical courses to practical courses? Though we have to be careful not to turn a biblical example into a biblical precept, it is instructive to note the "theoretical" nature of Paul's premissionary activity training. He was well acquainted with the Word. He was well acquainted with his times. This would suggest that our preministerial training today, with its attempt to give both a deep grounding in the Scriptures and a solid liberal arts background, is right on the mark. This is not to say that methods courses, for example, courses in preaching, teaching, evangelizing, counseling, and administration are unessential. It is to say that of prime importance is to present as candidates for the public ministry of the church men of God who have a good overall grasp of the Scriptures and an understanding of the world in which they are going to conduct their ministry. It is interesting to note how often the seminary faculty will receive notes from graduates who have been out for a few years and now want to express their gratitude for an education that gave them just those skills.

Third, we see the value of sending mature Christians out into the mission field. Think of the time that elapsed before the Holy Spirit told the church assembled at Antioch, "Set apart for me Barnabas and Saul for the work to which I have called them" (Acts 13:2). This was approximately 15 years after Paul's conversion. And Paul at his conversion was hardly unacquainted with the Scriptures. Nor was he an exceptionally young man. He was possibly in his early 30s at the time the risen Christ appeared to him on the Damascus road and thus about 45 when he began his missionary journeys.

It is true, of course, that other, younger men accompanied Paul, notably Timothy. John Mark was also, it appears, a young man. But Mark went along as a helper and Timothy, it seems clear, was closely supervised by Paul and only gradually entrusted with work that he would do independent of Paul's leadership.

Add to that Paul's own requirement that the overseer should not be a recent convert (1 Timothy 3:6), and we have some solid counsel to send out into the public ministry of the church those who are at least relatively mature in the faith.

Fourth, as we look at the Lord's preparation of Paul for his missionary career, *we note that the call sought the man and not vice versa.* It took a call of the church for him to begin his first missionary journey. On behalf of the congregation in Antioch, Barnabas called Paul into the ministry of the church at Antioch. And when, about a year later, Paul and Barnabas left on their first journey, it was the church at Antioch that "placed their hands on them and sent them off" (Acts 13:3).

The application of this truth to our ministry is nicely stated by Pastor Edgar Hoenecke in the essay "St. Paul's Missionary Approach to the Unchurched," delivered in 1963 to the Arizona-California Pastoral Conference:

> For this assignment into the world mission field St. Paul had waited for years, while he worked in comparative obscurity along the coast of the Mediterranean in Cilicia near his home city of Tarsus. . . .
>
> If the Lord wants to place us into a certain work, He will surely do so at His own good time and through the orderly process which He has established, through a call of the Church. In the meantime, our best preparation for whatever other post of duty the Lord has in mind for us is to exercise patience and faithfulness in the place and duty into which we have been called.[30]

1. Paul was a Jew by birth and upbringing. According to Jewish custom, Paul would have begun his study of the Scriptures at age 5. He would have begun to study Jewish customs at age 10 and become a "son of the covenant" (bar mitzvah) at age 13. What do we know about his early life from Scripture?

   - Acts 22:3 *from Tarsus, instructed by Gamiliel, Jew*

   - Acts 23:6 *Pharisee*

   - Acts 26:4,5; Galatians 1:14; Philippians 3:5,6
     Zealous for Jewish traditions /Judaism

2. Read Acts 22:2,3. Why was Paul's Jewish birth and upbringing an asset, for example, when he had to speak to the crowd in Jerusalem? *they knew he knew what he was talking about*

3. In addition to his religious studies, Paul learned a trade. What trade did he learn and how did it become important for his missionary work? See Acts 18:3; Acts 20:34; 1 Corinthians 4:12 (compare 9:6-15); 1 Thessalonians 2:9.
   tentmaking, gave him money (not a burden)

4. Paul grew up in Tarsus, the "Athens of the eastern Mediterranean," and learned Greek culture. What were important elements of Greek culture to which Paul was exposed?
   philosophy, poets

5. How did his understanding of Greek culture prove invaluable in his work of spreading the gospel? See Acts 17:28; 1 Corinthians 15:33; Titus 1:12. *Speak to Greeks*

6. Tarsus was a "free city," whose inhabitants, at least some of them, had been granted Roman citizenship. Why would Roman citizenship have been such a valuable status?
   gave him priveleges, saved his life at times

7. How did Paul's Roman citizenship become important for his missionary work? See Acts 16:37; 22:25-28; 25:11.
   Saved him

8. We learn about Paul's life from Luke's history in Acts and from Paul's own statements in Acts and in some of his letters. Below are references and dates to Paul's life before he began his first missionary journey. Trace this period of Paul's life by filling in the events. (Note: You may wish to create a time line and fill in the events on the time line instead of on the blanks.)

   A.D. 32—Acts 9:3-9 *Conversion*

   A.D. 32—Acts 9:19b-22 *preaching in Damascus*

A.D. 32–35—Galatians 1:15-17 *to Arabia*

A.D. 35—Galatians 1:18 *1ᵗ trip to Jerusalem*

A.D. 35–44—Acts 9:19b-30; Galatians 1:21 *to Syria & Cilicia*

A.D. 45—Acts 11:25,26 *to Antioch of Syria*

A.D. 46—Acts 11:27-30 *to Jerusalem for famine visit*

A.D. 46—Acts 12:25 *return from Jerusalem*

9. Paul was called to be an apostle. What was an apostle? Why was Paul an unusual candidate for apostleship? How was Paul received by the Jerusalem congregation? See Acts 22:17-21 and Acts 26:16-18. *— commissioned by God   — not liked*
— persecuted Christians

10. What effect did Paul's conversion have on his life? See Philippians 3:7-11 and 1 Timothy 1:15-17.
— recognized sin   — wanted to know Jesus

11. Through Paul's example the Lord teaches us about how he prepares people to be his witnesses. How do each of the following apply to Paul? Why is it important that witnesses share in these qualities and attitudes?

   • A changed heart is vital if one is to serve the Lord.
Want to do God's work
   • A witness needs a broad-based education.
helps us apply the Word
   • A witness knows that God works in his time, not necessarily in human time. *Know God is working through us*

   • God uses everything in a person's life to prepare that person to serve him. *bad things will turn good*

Part Three _____

Paul's Mission Strategy

AT THE END OF PART 2, it was noted that Paul, together with Barnabas, was serving the congregation in Antioch of Syria, the place where the disciples were first called Christians (Acts 11:26). In Part 3 of this study, we want to trace briefly what followed: the quite familiar course of Paul's three missionary journeys. Having done that, we want to see if we can discern the mission strategy that Paul followed. Then we want to determine what part of this strategy, if any, might be applicable to us today as we also seek to "make disciples of all nations" (Matthew 28:19).

We note right at the outset that the directive to begin what we today call the first missionary journey came from the Lord and that it came to a group of Christians whose desire was to be attuned to the Lord's will for them: "While they [the leaders in the church at Antioch, including Paul and Barnabas] were worshiping the Lord and fasting, the Holy Spirit said, 'Set apart for me Barnabas and Saul for the work to which I have called them'" (Acts 13:2). Likely the Spirit spoke through one of the leaders who had the gift of prophecy and who in turn would have revealed this message to the others (see 1 Corinthians 14:29-32; Acts 11:28; 21:11).

First journey, around A.D. *47 to 48 (Acts 13,14)*

Their first stop was the island of Cyprus, some 100 miles into the Mediterranean, southeast of Antioch. Did the Holy Spirit give them specific directions to begin at this particular place? It doesn't appear that this was the case. We are told that they were sent on their way by the Holy Spirit, probably a reference to the commissioning service at Antioch, which included prayer and fasting and laying on of hands (Acts 13:3,4); but we are not told that the Holy Spirit told them where to go.

It is more likely that they traveled to Cyprus because this seemed a logical place to begin. For one thing, Cyprus was the home of Barnabas. For another, the Christian gospel had already been proclaimed at least to a degree in Cyprus by some of the Jewish Christians who had been scattered after Stephen's martyrdom (Acts 11:19); so there would be a nucleus to work with. Another factor: There was a fairly sizeable number of Jews on the island of Cyprus, guaranteeing a synagogue in most Cypriot cities. One further reason for going to Cyprus may well have been its strategic location, situated as it was on the shipping lanes between Syria, Asia Minor, and Greece.

Cyprus, a senatorial as opposed to an imperial province, was administered by a proconsul, who was appointed by lot by the Roman senate and served in office for one year.[31] It was at Cyprus that Luke called Saul of Tarsus Paul for the first time (Acts 13:9) and also began to place his name before the name of Barnabas. In the future the only time he put the name of Barnabas first was when the two men were at the Jerusalem Council following the first journey (Acts 15:12), no doubt a recognition by Luke of Barnabas' standing in the Jerusalem church.

On Cyprus, as far as we are told, Paul and Barnabas preached the Word at two places only, the two key cities of the island. They began at the synagogue in Salamis on the east coast. Salamis was the most important city of the island and the administrative center for its eastern half. The capital of Cyprus, though, was the second city the missionaries visited, New Paphos, a Greek settlement 90 miles to the southwest of Salamis. Paphos was known for its shrine to Aphrodite. It was here that Paul and Barnabas brought the Word to the proconsul Sergius Paulus (around A.D. 46–48), at his invitation. It was here also that Paul confronted the sorcerer Elymas with the powerful Word of the Lord, which struck him blind for a time. We are told that when Sergius Paulus saw what happened, he believed. It wasn't the miracle that changed his life, though. Luke tells us that "he was amazed at the teaching about the Lord" (Acts 13:12; the NIV takes the genitive as an objective genitive: "teaching about the Lord" would be synonymous with "the Word of God" or "the gospel").

Moving on from there, Paul and Barnabas and John Mark, who had come along on the journey as an assistant, sailed to the mainland port of Perga in the province of Pamphylia. At this point John Mark returned home. Since Perga was the chief city in Pamphylia and Pamphylia did have some Jewish settlements, it is somewhat surprising that Paul spent very little time, as far as we know, evangelizing in Perga, though he did do so on the way back to Antioch (Acts 14:25).

William Ramsay spends quite a bit of time promoting the theory that Paul suffered from an attack of malaria in the lowlands of Pamphylia and so pushed on quickly to the higher altitude of Pisidian Antioch.[32] This, says Ramsay, is what Paul is referring to when he tells the Galatians, "It was because of an illness [in Greek, literally "a weakness of the flesh"] that I first preached the gospel to you" (Galatians 4:13). And this, Ramsay maintains, is Paul's "thorn in [the] flesh" (2 Corinthians 12:7). Not everyone agrees with Ramsay. Arndt-Gingrich lists several suggestions that various scholars have advanced as to the identity of Paul's thorn: epilepsy, hysteria, periodic depressions, headaches, severe eye trouble (Galatians 4:15), and a speech impediment.[33]

We aren't going to solve this problem here, nor do we have to do so in order to learn from it. Through his thorn in the flesh, whether it was connected with his visit to Perga or not, the Lord taught Paul that in a Christian's life obstacles are actually opportunities through which the Lord can carry out his work. "My grace is sufficient for you," he told Paul, "for my power is made perfect in weakness." Paul learned that lesson well. Think of his response:

"Therefore I will boast all the more gladly about my weaknesses, so that Christ's power may rest on me. That is why, for Christ's sake, I delight in weaknesses, in insults, in hardships, in persecutions, in difficulties. For when I am weak, then I am strong" (2 Corinthians 12:9,10).

Paul exemplifies a faith that is marked by trust in the promises of God, trust that, as he himself put it, "in all things God works for the good of those who love him, who have been called according to his purpose" (Romans 8:28). Those involved in mission work today, whether it be in this country or abroad, like Paul should not expect an obstacle-free ministry. Hostility, indifference, and meager results can discourage and depress. Faith, though, will cling to God's promises. It will not focus on what hasn't been done. It will not allow obstacles to lead one to conclude that it can't be done. Instead it will remember and treasure God's assurance that the gospel *is* the power of God for salvation and that it *will* accomplish what God desires and achieve the purpose for which he sent it (Romans 1:16; Isaiah 55:11).

Luke gives evidence of his careful work as a historian when he describes the next city that Paul visited as Pisidian Antioch. Actually this Antioch was in Phrygia, right on the border of Pisidia; but to distinguish it from another Antioch in Phrygia, it was commonly known as Pisidian Antioch. It was the most important city of the southern portion of the Roman province of Galatia, which formerly had consisted of the regions of eastern Phrygia, Pisidia, and western Lycaonia. In 25 B.C. Augustus had added these regions to the old kingdom of Galatia to the north and made this whole area into the province of Galatia.

Antioch was made a Roman colony in 6 B.C. to help protect Roman interests in the region. The great Roman road, the *Via Sebaste,* which stretched from Ephesus to the Euphrates, ran through the city. Antioch's population was a mixed one, made up of Greeks, Romans, native Phrygians, and Jews. According to Josephus, Antioch was one of the places where Antiochus III (223–187 B.C.) had settled Jews.[34] Paul, therefore, had no problem finding Jews. On the Sabbath, he and Barnabas entered the synagogue where he had the opportunity to address both Jews and God-fearing Gentiles (Acts 13:16).

Paul's message given in the synagogue in Antioch is the longest such message Luke has preserved for us. We will look at it in more detail in Part 4, when we explore Paul's mission messages. At this point we simply want to note that in Antioch a pattern began that was to be repeated often in Paul's travels: an initial acceptance of Paul and his message that was followed by strong resistance to and rejection of Paul on the part of some. "Many of the Jews and devout converts to Judaism [in Greek, literally "proselytes"] followed Paul and Barnabas," Luke tells us (Acts 13:43). But, then, on the next Sabbath, when almost the whole city had gathered to hear the Word of the Lord, "the Jews . . . were filled with jealousy and talked abusively against what Paul was saying" (Acts 13:45).

We do not have to conclude that the Jews mentioned in this verse are the same as those mentioned in verse 43. It appears, rather, that a congregation consisting of Jews and Gentiles was formed in Antioch, and it was a group of unbelieving Jews, joined later by some prominent Gentiles (Acts 13:50), that opposed Paul and Barnabas and expelled them from the city.

Before we leave Antioch, we should take note of one other significant point. Not only was a congregation established in Antioch, but "the word of the Lord spread through the whole region" (Acts 13:49). A better translation here for the word *spread* might be "was being carried" (the Greek verb form can be translated as an ongoing action in the past). The Word spreads when it is carried. Those who did the carrying of the Word aren't specified. The passive verb emphasizes what was happening rather than who was doing it. But the context suggests that the carriers weren't Paul and Barnabas but rather those in Antioch to whom these two missionaries brought the gospel.

The next stop, Iconium, about 80 miles from Antioch, was an ancient Phrygian town that had been transformed by the Greeks into a city-state. Though under Rome, it remained strongly Greek in character. Ramsay calls it the Damascus of Asia Minor because, like Damascus, it was blessed with much water, a good climate, rich vegetation, and great prosperity.

Again it was the synagogue to which Paul and Barnabas went first, and again "a great number of Jews and Gentiles believed" (Acts 14:1). And, as at Antioch, "the Jews who refused to believe stirred up the Gentiles and poisoned their minds against the brothers" (Acts 14:2). In time Paul and Barnabas were forced to leave; but not before, even in the face of stiff opposition, they had "spent considerable time there, speaking boldly for the Lord" (Acts 14:3).

Lystra, their next stop, was only 20 miles from Iconium, but it was in another district of Galatia. Lystra and Derbe are called Lycaonian cities by Luke (Acts 14:6), further evidence of Luke's historical accuracy. (Ramsay notes the fact that between A.D. 37 and 72, and at no other time, Iconium was on the Phrygian side of the regional border between Phrygia and Lycaonia.[35])

Lystra was an ancient Lycaonian village turned into a Roman colony by Augustus in 6 B.C. He brought Roman soldiers and their families into the city, making it the easternmost of the fortified cities of Galatia. Though the ruling class was made up mostly of Roman army veterans, the population consisted chiefly of uneducated Lycaonians, who spoke their own language.

Apparently there were not many Jews in Lystra, although it appears to have been the home of Timothy (Acts 16:1-3). At least we have no record of Paul preaching in the synagogue. Paul rather appears to have done his evangelizing in the open air, where a certain lame man listened to him and was healed by Paul. Following this healing there came another of the addresses of Paul that we plan to look at later.

It was also in Lystra that Paul was stoned and left for dead by the mob that was aroused by unbelieving Jews who had followed him from Antioch and Iconium. From there Paul moved on to his final stop on the first journey, Derbe, about 60 miles from Lystra. Derbe was in the southeastern part of the Lycaonian region of Galatia and the home of the Gaius mentioned in Acts 20:4, who was among those who went back with Paul to Jerusalem with the offering gathered for the needy believers there.

Paul was blessed with good results in Derbe: "They preached the good news in that city and won a large number of disciples" (Acts 14:21); but we know nothing of the composition of the congregation that was formed.

We will leave discussion of the final part of Paul's first journey, his return to strengthen and encourage the believers of the congregations he had founded, to our final essay, which will look at Paul's follow-up. At this point we skip over this and take note of the fact that the journey ends where it began, in Antioch of Syria, the place "where they had been committed to the grace of God for the work they had now completed" (Acts 14:26). This was the calling body; so to this group of believers they brought their report. Note how it is worded. Paul and Barnabas didn't speak of their successes, of how everything worked out according to their plans. Rather, they reported "all that God had done through them and how he had opened the door of faith to the Gentiles" (Acts 14:27).

Second journey, around A.D. 49 to 52 (Acts 15:36–18:22)

Though the Jerusalem Council, which took place around A.D. 49, between the first and second journeys of Paul (Acts 15:1-35), was of great importance to the early church, for the sake of time, we are going to pass it by and move on to Paul's second journey. We want to continue to focus on the places to which Paul traveled and the people to whom he brought the gospel to see if we can discern any pattern that would suggest a predetermined mission strategy on Paul's part.

Though Paul saw himself by the Lord's commission as called primarily to "plant" new churches (see Romans 15:20 and 2 Corinthians 10:16), his words to Barnabas at the outset of the second journey remind us that he also had a shepherd's heart. "Let us go back and visit the brothers in all the towns where we preached the word of the Lord," he suggested to Barnabas, "and see how they are doing" (Acts 15:36). The disagreement that arose at that time between Paul and Barnabas as to the advisability of giving John Mark another chance is well known. When they could not agree, they went their separate ways, Barnabas taking his cousin Mark and returning to Cyprus. With that Barnabas passes out of the picture of Acts; but Mark, the young man he encouraged, turned out to be a good investment of Barnabas' time and energy. As Mark matured he became a valued helper of both Paul and Peter in their later years and, probably sometime shortly after A.D. 65, wrote the gospel that bears his name. (See Colossians 4:10; 2 Timothy 4:11; Philemon 24; 1 Peter 5:13.) Justin Martyr (died 165) called the gospel of Mark the memoirs of Peter.

Paul, then, chose another companion, Silas (Acts 15:40), who is also known as Silvanus (see NIV text note at 1 Thessalonians 1:1; 2 Thessalonians 1:1), which was probably his Roman surname. Silas apparently was a highly respected member of the Jerusalem congregation since he was one of the two men asked to convey to the church at Antioch the decisions of the Jerusalem Council (Acts 15:22). He was also, along with Paul, a Roman citizen (Acts 16:36,37).

Silas was, as it turned out, one of three men who accompanied Paul on at least parts of his second journey. In revisiting the cities of southern Galatia that had been evangelized on the first journey, Paul came to Lystra and there invited Timothy, the son of a gentile father and Jewish mother, to accompany him and Silas. It was at least in part on the basis of the recommendation of the congregations in Lystra and Iconium that Paul extended this invitation. He first had Timothy circumcised to avoid giving offense to the Jews of the area who knew that his father was a Greek (Acts 16:1-3).

Having revisited the Galatian churches, where was Paul to go next? The logical step would be to extend the gospel to the province immediately to the west, to Asia, another senatorial province. Asia consisted largely of the old kingdom of Pergamum. Pergamum's last king, Attalus III, had in 133 B.C. bequeathed his kingdom to Rome in return for Rome's agreement to allow the city of Pergamum and other Greek cities in the area to remain free from tribute.

Paul's plan, apparently, was to bring the gospel to Asia, possibly to the cities along the *Via Sebaste*, which ended in Ephesus. But he was "kept by the Holy Spirit from preaching the word in the province of Asia" (Acts 16:6). He turned north, therefore, with the intention of heading into the senatorial province of Bithynia and its important cities along the Black Sea, all of which were connected by an elaborate road system. But at the border of Mysia, the northern region of the province of Asia, the Lord again intervened. "They tried to enter Bithynia, but the Spirit of Jesus would not allow them to" (Acts 16:7).

In this way, by a process of elimination, Paul ended up where the Lord wanted him to be, at Troas, on the eastern shore of the Aegean Sea. Troas was a seaport once controlled by the Greeks. After the break-up of Alexander the Great's empire, it fell into the hands of the Seleucids. At Paul's time it was a Roman colony. It is here that the "we" narrative of Acts begins (Acts 16:10), an indication that Luke had joined the missionary team as a fourth member. Luke evidently remained with Paul until Paul left Philippi on his second journey. He then rejoined Paul when Paul returned to Philippi at the close of his third journey. Thereafter Luke appears to have been a constant companion of Paul.

Compare Acts 16:40, where Luke tells us that *they* (that is, Paul and Silas) left Philippi, with Acts 20:6, where Luke states that *we* sailed from Philippi and joined the others at Troas. Luke then accompanied Paul on his final trip to Jerusalem (Acts 20,21). He was with him on his voyage to Rome (Acts 27), and he was with Paul during both his first and second imprisonments (Colossians 4:14; 2 Timothy 4:11; Philemon 24).

Troas, though, is remembered for more than being the city where Luke joined Paul, Silas, and Timothy. Of more significance is that in Troas, Paul, in a vision, received the "Macedonian call." He and his companions concluded that this call, "Come over to Macedonia and help us," could have had only one source and one meaning. It was God himself who was telling them to cross the Aegean into Europe and to bring the people there the greatest help anyone could bring, the help afforded by the gospel (Acts 16:9,10).

Paul visited three cities in Macedonia: Philippi, Thessalonica, and Berea. Philippi, on the *Via Egnatia*, the road that stretched from Byzantium in the east to the Adriatic Sea on the west, was a strategic commercial center. Luke calls it "the leading city of that district of Macedonia" (Acts 16:12; Macedonia had been divided into four districts by the Romans). Philippi was a Roman colony administered by two chief magistrates. (See Acts 16:20. Here the word *magistrate* would be "praetor" in Latin. This is yet another example of Luke's accurate reporting as he keeps straight the different ways by which Rome administered its conquered territories.) As was often the case with Roman colonies, a large contingent of Roman army veterans called Philippi home.

There appeared to be an anti-Semitic spirit in Philippi, at least on the part of some. When the owners of the slave girl out of whom Paul drove the evil spirit brought Paul and Silas before the magistrates, their charge was, "These men are *Jews*, and are throwing our city into an uproar by advocating customs unlawful for us Romans to accept or practice" (Acts 16:20,21, italics added).

There were very few Jews in Philippi, not enough, it appears, to start a synagogue, which required but ten men. So Paul had to alter his normal approach, but he still went first to those who had some connection with Judaism. On the Sabbath he went to a place along the river where, apparently, he had been told that the Jews gathered for prayer. One convert, the God-fearing Lydia, provided a place for Paul and his three companions to stay.

We know very little else about Paul's work in Philippi except for his evangelizing and baptizing the jailer and his family. But we are given a clear indication that Paul's work there did bear fruit. After their release from prison, we are told that Paul and Silas "went to Lydia's house, where they met with the brothers and encouraged them" (Acts 16:40). These "brothers" apparently had been brought into the church through what we today might call raw mission work, though there may well have been more God worshipers and proselytes in Philippi than Lydia, who were led by the Spirit through Paul's gospel preaching to trust in Jesus as the Messiah and their Savior. Other Philippian believers are mentioned by name in Paul's letter to the church at Philippi: Epaphroditus, Euodia, Syntyche, and Clement.

It was a different story in Thessalonica, about one hundred miles southwest of Philippi. It was the largest and most prosperous city of Macedonia, the capital of another of the four administrative districts of the province, as well as the capital of all of Macedonia. Thessalonica had a substantial Jewish population. Paul, therefore, could begin his ministry there in the synagogue, where he spoke on three Sabbath days. Again the gospel proved itself to be the power of God for the salvation of both Jews and Greeks, although it appears that especially the Gentiles in the synagogue were receptive to the gospel. Luke tells us, "*Some* of the Jews were persuaded and joined Paul and Silas, as did *a large number* of God-fearing Greeks and *not a few* prominent women" (Acts 17:4, italics added). Evidently Paul spent time also working among the heathen in Thessalonica, since in writing to the church at Thessalonica, he said, "You turned to God *from idols* to serve the living and true God" (1 Thessalonians 1:9, italics added).

Jealousy on the part of the unbelieving Jews cut short Paul's stay in Thessalonica. Jason, in whose home Paul and Silas appeared to have stayed, was required to post a bond to the city officials. (The word the NIV translates as "city officials" is literally "politarchs." Ancient inscriptions reveal that a body of five such politarchs ruled Thessalonica. Again we see Luke the historian at work.) This bond was most likely intended as some kind of guarantee that Paul would no longer preach in Thessalonica (Acts 17:5-9).

His new Christian friends brought him to Berea, some 50 miles southwest of Thessalonica. Berea was in a third district of Macedonia, though not it but Pella was the chief city of that district. And Berea wasn't on the main road, the *Via Egnatia*. It is quite possible that this was not a part of Paul's planned itinerary, but that he ended up there because that is where he was sent by the brothers in Thessalonica for safety's sake. ("In a fervent speech against Piso, Cicero [106–43 B.C.] told how the Roman authorities in Thessalonica were so unpopular with the people that, when he was on government business, he found it wise to sneak into the provincial capital at night and at times withdraw from the storm of complaints to Berea because it was 'off the beaten track.'")[36]

Whatever the cause of his visit to Berea, it was certainly blessed by God. We are told that Paul and Silas "went to the Jewish synagogue" and that "many of the Jews believed, as did a number of prominent Greek women and many Greek men" (Acts 17:10, 12). Luke is usually careful to identify Greeks as "God fearing" or proselytes if he wants us to see them as persons who, to a certain degree, were connected with the synagogue. But even though Luke doesn't identify them that way here, the sentence structure is such that it would appear that these Greek men and women were among those to whom Paul preached in the synagogue.

The unbelieving Thessalonian Jews, not content to have pushed Paul out of their city, followed him to Berea. Concern for his safety led the "brothers" in Berea to personally escort Paul all the way to Athens. Again, this does not seem to be part of a pre-arranged itinerary but, rather, the attempt of friends to get Paul far away from the Jews of Macedonia who were relentless in their pursuit. Athens, a five-day voyage from Berea, was also in a different province, that of Achaia.

Athens, conquered by Rome in 146 B.C., had been given the status of a free city. Though it had reached its peak in the fifth century B.C., it was still the cultural and intellectual center of Greece. In other respects, though, it had been far eclipsed by Corinth, the capital of Achaia. The population of Athens at this time is estimated to be only about ten thousand. Corinth, on the other hand, was the fourth largest city in the Roman Empire, with a population of about 250,000.

Only Paul was forced to leave Berea; Silas and Timothy remained there. The men who escorted Paul to Athens returned to Berea with the request of Paul for Silas and Timothy to rejoin him in Athens. But Paul didn't sit by idly while waiting for their arrival. Instead he did mission work in two places: "He reasoned in the synagogue with the Jews and the God-fearing Greeks, as well as in the *marketplace* day by day with those who happened to be there" (Acts 17:17, italics added).

Luke gives us the address Paul gave when he was invited to appear before the Areopagus, probably a board or review committee that made judgments on matters of public teaching, an address that we will examine when we look at Paul's mission messages. At this point we will take note only of the fact that, though Paul's outward success in Athens was apparently the most limited of any of the places he visited, yet at least one of the members of the Areopagus, Dionysius, along with a woman named Damaris and "a number of others" (Acts 17:34), who may have been Jews or Gentiles, became believers. As far as we know, however, no congregation was formed in Athens at this time.

Paul's final second-journey destination was Corinth, situated on the narrow isthmus between Attica to the north and the Peloponnisos to the south. It was an ancient city already at Paul's time. Archaeologists have discovered remains from the third millennium B.C. Homer in the *Illiad*, around 1200 B.C., called the city "wealthy Corinth." In 146 B.C. the Romans destroyed the city, and in 46 B.C. it was reestablished by Julius Caesar. It was the seat of the Roman proconsul who, from Corinth, administered the senatorial province of Achaia.

Corinth was a center of commerce. A mainland east-west route passed through it, and several sea routes converged on its two harbors: Cenchrea on the east and Lechaeum on the west. Cargo was hauled by land across the narrow isthmus. In some cases, if the ship was small enough, the whole ship was pulled overland on a system of rollers from one side of the isthmus to the other.

Corinth's reputation for immorality was well known. Its temple of Aphrodite had more than one thousand female prostitutes. If a Corinthian was shown on stage in a Greek play, he or she generally was portrayed as a drunk or a prostitute. The verb *to corinthianize* found its way into the Greek language, meaning to live like a Corinthian in the practice of sexual immorality.

It was in Corinth that Paul met fellow Jews and tent makers, Aquila and Priscilla, who had been forced out of Rome because of Emperor Claudius' decree, around A.D. 51, that all Jews must leave Rome. And it was also in Corinth that Paul was rejoined by Silas and Timothy, whom he had sent from Athens back to Macedonia (see 1 Thessalonians 3:1-6).

We remember Corinth for a number of reasons. At Corinth the proconsul Gallio[37] ruled that Christianity was in effect merely a sect of Judaism, hence a *religio licita*. At Corinth the Lord in a vision graciously gave Paul a personal word of encouragement, much needed after a rather discouraging time in Athens and after having been forced to leave each of the cities he had visited in Macedonia. The Lord told him: "Do not be afraid; keep on speaking, do not be silent. For I am with you, and no one is going to attack and harm you, because I have many people in this city" (Acts 18:9,10).

But we remember Corinth especially as a place where the Lord permitted Paul to remain for a year and a half, the second longest stay we know of in his missionary journeys. During this time the gospel spread beyond Corinth, as Paul indicates when he begins his second letter to Corinth with the greeting, "To the church of God in Corinth, together with all the saints throughout Achaia" (2 Corinthians 1:1). In Romans, written from Corinth at the close of his third journey, Paul mentions by name one of those saints in Achaia outside Corinth: Phoebe, who was from Cenchrea (Romans 16:1).

He began his work in Corinth in the place where, if at all possible, he always began: "Every Sabbath he reasoned in the synagogue, trying to persuade Jews and Greeks" (Acts 18:4). But when

Jewish opposition and abuse made it impossible for him to continue there, he went next door to the house of the gentile "God-fearer" Titius Justus and apparently used his home as the base from which he now brought the gospel to the pagan Gentiles. His synagogue preaching did bear at least some fruit, however. The ruler of the synagogue himself, Crispus, and his whole family became believers. The greeting in 1 Corinthians 1:1, "Paul, called to be an apostle of Christ Jesus by the will of God, and our brother Sosthenes," indicates that the successor of Crispus, Sosthenes (Acts 18:17), may also have become a follower of Christ, although we cannot be sure that the same Sosthenes is meant in both passages.

After a brief stop in Ephesus, across the Aegean Sea from Corinth, where he "went into the synagogue and reasoned with the Jews" (Acts 18:19), Paul left Aquila and Priscilla and returned to his home base of Antioch in Syria, after visiting the church in Jerusalem (Acts 18:22). He spent some time there, possibly parts of A.D. 52 and 53, and then set off on what we today call his third journey.

Third journey, around A.D. 53 to 57 (Acts 18:23–21:17)

The third journey is different from the first two in that Paul did not plant the seed in as much untouched soil as before. He spent the majority of his time in one place, Ephesus, prefaced by another visit to the churches of Galatia and concluded with a revisit of the churches in Macedonia and Achaia.

It is in Ephesus that we meet Apollos for the first time. For our purposes it is sufficient to note that, though Paul is certainly the key man, he did not lack helpers. It was the husband and wife team, Aquila and Priscilla, who filled in the gaps of Apollos' knowledge of the gospel (Acts 18:26). And then it was Apollos who built on Paul's foundation in Corinth or, to use Paul's picture, who watered what Paul had planted (1 Corinthians 3:6). Luke tells us that Apollos went to Corinth from Ephesus with a letter of recommendation from the believers in Ephesus, and that in Corinth "he was a great help to those who by grace had believed. For he vigorously refuted the Jews in public debate, proving from the Scriptures that Jesus was the Christ" (Acts 18:27,28).

Ephesus was the capital and most important city of the Roman province of Asia, founded in the 12th or 11th century B.C. by Ionian colonists from Athens. From 133 B.C. it had been under Roman rule. Situated at the mouth of the Cayster River, it was a seaport, but by New Testament times, its importance as a trading center had diminished somewhat because the harbor kept on getting filled with silt.

Its greatest claim to fame was its temple for the worship of the multibreasted fertility goddess Artemis. The temple, supported by 127 columns, each 60 feet high, was one of the seven wonders of the ancient world. It was four times the size of the Parthenon in Athens.

The Lord gave Paul much time in Ephesus, three months in the synagogue, where he was "arguing persuasively about the kingdom of God" (Acts 19:8); and then, when the usual opposition arose, he took the new believers with him and taught daily in the lecture hall of Tyrannus. "This went on for two years," Luke tells us (Acts 19:10). In his farewell to the Ephesian elders, Paul reminds them, "For three years I never stopped warning each of you night and day" (Acts 20:31). This is Paul's longest stay in any one place that we know of. The Greek word translated "warning" means "to put in the mind," then "to admonish, exhort, urge, warn."

Once again, it appears that the nucleus for the congregation at Ephesus came out of the synagogue but that it didn't stop with this nucleus. Luke, in fact, tells us that during the time that Paul was teaching in the lecture hall of Tyrranus, "all the Jews and Greeks who lived in the province of Asia heard the word of the Lord" (Acts 19:10). This was likely the time during which the other congregations of Asia were founded, notably the churches mentioned in Revelation chapters 2 and 3.

Paul's stay in Ephesus was unusual in another respect. As in Corinth, he did not leave because he was forced to leave, though the riot stirred up by Demetrius the silversmith did occur right at the time Paul had planned to take his leave of Ephesus. Luke tells us: "Paul decided to go to Jerusalem, passing through Macedonia and Achaia. 'After I have been there,' he said, 'I must visit Rome also'" (Acts 19:21). The Greek here may indicate that Paul's plans were determined by the Holy Spirit or, at least, that he was guided by the Spirit in his itinerary. Paul's intention was not to do mission work in Rome, which had already been evangelized, but to use

Rome as a base of operations for the evangelization of Spain. After leaving Ephesus, he wrote to the Romans from Corinth:

> Now that there is no more place for me to work in these regions, and since I have been longing for many years to see you, I plan to do so when I go to Spain. I hope to visit you while passing through and to have you assist me on my journey there, after I have enjoyed your company for a while. Now, however, I am on my way to Jerusalem in the service of the saints there. For Macedonia and Achaia were pleased to make a contribution for the poor among the saints in Jerusalem. So after I have completed this task . . . , I will go to Spain and visit you on the way. (Romans 15:23-26,28)

We do not know for sure whether Paul did get to Spain, a distance of about 2,300 miles! The epistle of Clement (A.D. 96) speaks of Paul reaching the limits of the West (Spain?) with the gospel. This visit would have taken place sometime following Paul's release from his first imprisonment in Rome. Acts ends before this release, a release that the pastoral epistles assume.

We know, however, that the Scriptures record no further pioneering mission work of Paul's after Ephesus. Following his revisit of the churches in Macedonia and Achaia, Paul traveled to Jerusalem with the offering. He was imprisoned in Caesarea for two years, after which, because of his appeal to stand before Caesar, he was put on board a ship to Rome, where he was imprisoned for another two years. And with that, Acts comes to an end.

Summary of Paul's strategy

In this brief review of Paul's journeys, we have been on the lookout for clues to Paul's mission strategy. A number of factors suggest themselves:

1. Paul was flexible in his itinerary.

This is not to say that his journeys were more or less an aimless wandering as he waited for some kind of signal from the Lord as to where to go. His general goal was "to preach the gospel where Christ was not known" (Romans 15:20). He also made specific plans to fulfill this goal. On his journeys he was sent out by the Lord through the church, but in general his itinerary does not appear to have been determined directly by the Lord. Undoubtedly it was he and Barnabas who decided to make Cyprus the first stop on the first journey and then to sail to Perga and to bring the gospel to Galatia. On his second journey, Paul apparently had determined to preach the gospel in the province of Asia. At the end of his second journey, he told the Ephesians that he would come back and spend more time with them. He did just that. And at the end of his third journey, he didn't return to Ephesus but, rather, had the Ephesian elders come out to the coast to meet him, because this was in keeping with his plan to get to Jerusalem in time for the day of Pentecost (Acts 20:16). And always in the back of his mind was his long-range goal to bring the gospel to Spain.

There appears to be order and direction, then, in Paul's travels, but there was no rigidity. We note two evidences of Paul's flexibility. One was his openness to the Lord's leading. When the Lord directed his steps to Troas and from Troas to Macedonia and thus away from the evangelization of Asia at that time, Paul willingly adapted his plans to the Lord's direction. He fully realized that it is the Lord, not man, who opens doors, and that therefore God's plans had priority over his.

Then there was Paul's response to setbacks and opposition. When, as a result of his persecution in Thessalonica, he was brought to Berea, and then, as a result of persecution in Berea, he was brought to Athens, he didn't grumble about how the unfortunate circumstances had put a crimp into his plans. He simply went to work preaching where he was. And when his trip to Rome didn't turn out as he had planned, at least not for some time, he spent the two years there, not complaining about the way things never work out as expected but preaching the kingdom of God and teaching about the Lord Jesus Christ.

This would suggest to us today the need to strike a proper balance between careful planning and goal-setting in both our home and world mission work and a wholesome flexibility that is open to the leading of the Lord. It is not Paul but another of the pillars of the church, James the Lord's brother, who warns us not to be overconfident about our own plans: "Now listen, you who say, 'Today or tomorrow we will go to this or that city, spend a year there, carry on business and make money.' Why, you do not even know what will happen tomorrow" (James 4:13,14).

We can become so caught up in things like five-year or ten-year plans that we fail to catch the gentle nudging of the Lord to move in directions different from what we have plotted. "Macedonian calls" can still occur today in both the home and world mission fields. Not every call is the call of God, of course, but the Lord can still lead his church in this way. The newly converted Paul's humble petition "What shall I do, Lord?" is a good prayer for mission planners today as they seek to chart out the mission thrust of our church body in the years to come.

2. *Paul carried on his work largely in the most strategic cities of an area.*

Of the 13 cities mentioned by name in which Paul worked during his three journeys, all but Berea and possibly Lystra and Derbe fit into this category. And even these cities were not insignificant. Though Pella was the most important city in the third district of Macedonia, in New Testament times Berea was a large city. And though Lystra and Derbe were not as large and influential as Antioch and Iconium, they were the chief cities in the Lycaonian district of the province of Galatia.

As we have seen, the cities to which Paul brought the gospel were generally commercial centers. They were on main trade routes; nearly all of them were on the most important highways connecting east and west. They were key provincial cities. They were places where diverse ethnic and cultural groups lived and to which they traveled and intermingled. For the most part, as far as we know, Paul did not work in the interior of the provinces but confined his efforts to these key urban centers.

Paul evidently saw these cities as hubs from which the gospel could radiate into the rest of the provinces. That is exactly what appears to have happened. He preached the gospel in Antioch of Pisidia, and "the word of the Lord spread through the whole region" (Acts 13:49). He preached the gospel in Thessalonica, and the Lord's message rang out from there into the rest of Macedonia and even into Achaia and beyond (1 Thessalonians 1:8). He preached the gospel in Corinth, and it spread into the surrounding province of Achaia (2 Corinthians 1:1; Romans 16:1). He preached the gospel in Ephesus, and "all the Jews and Greeks who lived in the province of Asia heard the word of the Lord" as "the word of the Lord spread widely" (Acts 19:10,20). Paul thus evangelized whole provinces or regions of provinces by evangelizing the strategic city of the province or region.

In our day cities are, if anything, even more strategically important for mission work than they were in the days of Saint Paul—but not for exactly the same reasons. Today the strategic importance of cities is seen more in terms of the number of people flocking into them than of those moving out from them into other areas. Consider the following statistics that illustrate the movement of population in the United States from rural to urban areas:[38]

Year	Urban (in millions)	Percent	Rural (in millions)	Percent
1890	22.1	35.1	40.8	64.9
1940	74.4	56.5	57.2	43.5
1990	187.1	75.2	61.7	24.8

Who are these people flocking to the cities? A large number of them are of cultures different from those with which congregations of the WELS historically have carried out their ministries.

A goodly percentage of these people of different cultures are recent immigrants. Robert Samelson, a contributing editor to *Newsweek* magazine and columnist for *The Washington Post*, in an editorial that appeared May 4, 2000, in the *Milwaukee Journal Sentinel*, talked about the effect that immigration is having on our nation. He mentioned that the Census Bureau projects that by 2025 immigrants will comprise 12 percent of the population of the United States and that their American-born children will conservatively comprise another 12 to 13 percent. That's about 25 percent, one fourth of the population of the United States projected to be immigrants or first generation children of immigrants just 25 years from now. And most of them are settling in the cities of our nation.

Where are these immigrants coming from? In 1970, 62 percent of all immigrants were from Europe and 9 percent from Canada (about seven out of ten immigrants). Originating in Europe and Canada, these were more or less "our kind of people." In 1997, however, 51 percent of immigrants came from Latin America and 27 percent from Asia. Almost eight out of ten immigrants today are no longer our kind of people. Most important, they are people who do not know God, or if they do, they do not know what he has done for them. What a potential mission field this immigrant population is!

As a church body, doing mission work in the city has not been our strong point. In the earlier days of our synod, we were fairly well represented in a few large cities, Milwaukee, Wisconsin, most notably; but we were conducting our work mainly among our own people—German immigrants and their children. When they moved out of the city and people of other races and cultures replaced them, our churches, for the most part, experienced a drastic decline in membership.

In recent years, by the grace of God, we have experienced a reverse in this decline, at least in some areas, as we have begun to learn how to work with different cultural and racial groups. Yet, with only a few exceptions, we are still only marginally represented in the largest cities of our nation. Clearly, since the cities are home to such vast numbers of people of every nation, tribe, language, and people, cities should be of strategic importance when planning the deployment of workers and allocation of monies.

The same holds true on the world mission field. Of the 15 largest cities in the world, 13 are outside the United States and are projected to keep growing, often at a phenomenal rate, as the following chart indicates:[39]

Rank	City	1995 Estimated Population (in millions)	2015 Projected Population (in millions)	Percent Increase
1	Tokyo, Japan	27.0	28.9	7.2
2	Mexico City, Mexico	16.6	19.2	15.8
3	São Paulo, Brazil	16.5	20.3	22.9
5	Mumbai (Bombay), India	15.1	26.2	73.2
6	Shanghai, China	13.6	18.0	32.3
8	Calcutta, India	11.9	17.3	45.1
9	Buenos Aires, Argentina	11.8	13.9	17.4
10	Seoul, South Korea	11.6	13.0	11.8
11	Beijing, China	11.3	15.6	37.8
12	Osaka, Japan	10.6	10.6	0
13	Lagos, Nigeria	10.3	24.7	139.5
14	Rio de Janeiro, Brazil	10.2	11.9	16.5
15	Delhi, India	9.9	16.8	69.5

To do mission work we need to go where the people are, even though the work may be difficult and the results meager. In some cases the WELS Board for World Missions recognized the strategic importance of the cities right from day one. Our mission work in Japan began in Tokyo; in Taiwan, it began in Taipei. We went first to Jakarta in Indonesia, to Porto Alegre in Brazil, Medellin and Bogota in Colombia, Santa Domingo in the Dominican Republic, Novosibirsk in Russia, Sofia in Bulgaria, Chiang Mai in Thailand.

In other areas the work began in the more rural areas but then moved to more intensive work in the larger cities, such as Mexico

City, Mexico; San Juan, Puerto Rico; and Lusaka, Zambia. Though in certain ways mission work may be easier and produce more visible fruits in rural areas, those who know that Christ died for all will not neglect the masses of humanity moving to and living in big cities, both at home and abroad.

3. *Paul's work in the synagogue served as a bridge to the community.*

We have already touched on this in Part 1 of this study, but we are coming back to it here because it was an essential part of Paul's overall mission strategy. If there was a synagogue in the city, that is the place where Paul, apparently without exception, began his work.

One reason, certainly, was the unique position of the Jews in God's plan of salvation. Paul tells the Romans:

> Theirs is the adoption as sons; theirs the divine glory, the covenants, the receiving of the law, the temple worship and the promises. Theirs are the patriarchs, and from them is traced the human ancestry of Christ, who is God over all, forever praised! Amen. (Romans 9:4,5)

It was only right, therefore, that the gospel should first be offered to the Jews (Acts 13:46). But Paul did not look upon this simply as an obligation. His heart went out to his fellow Jews. "I could wish that I myself were cursed and cut off from Christ," he says, "for the sake of my brothers, those of my own race, the people of Israel" (Romans 9:3,4).

There may well have been yet another reason, however, for Paul's heading to the synagogue as soon as he entered a city. By doing so he could begin his work where he would be most likely to receive at least an initial hearing—and not just from the Jews. Ramsay reminds us that by inaugurating his mission work in a synagogue of the community, Paul also "was always sure of a good opening for his Gentile mission among the 'God-fearing,' who formed part of his audience in every synagogue."[40]

In the synagogue he found people, both Jews and Gentiles, who were acquainted with the Old Testament and were at least somewhat cognizant of the messianic prophecies. Paul could build upon that knowledge and point them to Jesus as the fulfillment of those prophecies.

The result? Within a relatively short period of time, the Holy Spirit could bring into existence a fellowship of believers, a Christian congregation, which could then serve as the nucleus to work with Paul in bringing the gospel of Jesus to the people around them.

In no case that we know of did Paul fail to gather such a congregation of believers, even though his major work generally came to be outside the synagogue because the opposition of unbelieving Jews eventually forced him to leave the synagogue. The initial work in the synagogue turned out to be the bridge to bring the gospel to a wider audience.

The Lord provides similar bridges today. It is possible that we do not appreciate them as highly as we should, for quite often they cause considerable problems. It is not difficult to document that many an original nucleus, whether on the home or the world mission field, turned out to be a bitter disappointment, for example, an obstructionist little nucleus in a home mission congregation that bitterly opposes anything that threatens the status quo, causing the missionary no end of grief. We will want to remember that Paul's synagogue experiences were not of the "they lived happily ever after" variety either. They did, however, provide a way into the community.

So it is today. These nuclei, weak and frail as they sometimes are, serve as bridges to the community.

In this way Paul started wherever he could. It is the way the Lord provides entrance into many a mission field yet today.

4. *Right from the beginning, Paul established heterogeneous churches.*

When Paul entered the synagogue, he faced a heterogeneous group of Jews and of gentile "God-fearers" or proselytes. The congregations that were formed as a result of his synagogue preaching were similarly composed. Again and again that pattern was repeated, for example, in Berea: "Some of the Jews [of the synagogue] were persuaded and joined Paul and Silas, as did a large number of God-fearing Greeks and not a few prominent women"

(Acts 17:4). We might also add the fact that the church which sent out Paul and Barnabas on their journeys, Antioch of Syria, was likewise a heterogeneous church, a blending of Jews and Gentiles.

One of the strongest contentions of the Church Growth Movement is that the church grows best when the gospel is brought to homogeneous groups and when homogeneous, rather than heterogeneous, congregations are organized. If there is any one principle that is the distinguishing mark of the Church Growth Movement in the writings of its "father," Donald McGavran, it is this homogeneous unit principle. McGavran bases it on a faulty exegesis of Matthew 28:19, where he interprets "all nations" as each homogeneous unit in society, the "castes, tribes, peoples, ethnic units of mankind."[41] The world is a mosaic, McGavran contends, consisting of a very large number, perhaps tens of thousands, of homogeneous units, and "if God's plan for the salvation of the world is to be carried out, a mighty multiplication of living congregations must occur in most pieces of the mosaic in most countries."[42]

This principle undergirds McGavran's whole approach to church growth. C. Peter Wagner, after defining a homogeneous unit as "a group of people who consider each other to be 'our kind of people,'" writes: "Of all the scientific hypotheses developed within the Church Growth framework, this one [the homogeneous unit principle] as nearly as any approaches a 'law.' Show me a growing church, and I will show you a homogeneous unit."[43] McGavran writes:

> The Christian Faith will spread better if it takes account of distinguishable pieces of the mosaic, and encourages the multiplication of churches *in each piece*. Becoming a Christian . . . must not mean leaving *that* segment of society and joining *this*. Rather it must mean remaining in that piece of the mosaic and there living the life of the new creation.[44]
>
> There is no other way in which the multitudinous pieces of the human mosaic can become Christian. . . . Requiring converts to join conglomerate congregations will hinder the church from rapidly spreading to [all the nations].[45]
>
> Men like to become Christians without crossing racial, linguistic, or class barriers.[46]

In most cases of arrested growth of the Church, men are deterred not so much by the offense of the cross as by non-biblical offenses [for example, requiring people to cross linguistic, class, or racial barriers].[47]

The greatest obstacles to conversion are social, not theological.[48]

McGavran speculates that the Jews, who "liked to become Christian without crossing racial barriers," stopped becoming Christians once Gentiles predominated and they had to join a "house church full of Gentiles. So they turned sorrowfully away."[49] It is also his opinion that in the initial turnings to the Christian faith in northern Europe, failure to follow the principle "that men like to become Christian without crossing barriers kept whole countries out of eternal life for centuries."[50]

Like his mentor McGavran, C. Peter Wagner is guilty of some faulty exegesis in his attempt to use Scriptures to back up the homogeneous unit principle. He states that research "has shown reasonably conclusively that evangelistic efforts based on the notion that all kinds of people should be encouraged to join the same local congregation are generally ineffective"; and then he seeks to support this contention with this appeal from the Scriptures:

> Conglomerate congregations, . . . Acts 6:1-7 seems to be teaching us, were generally not feasible. . . . Paul's Epistles and the Jerusalem Council (Acts 15) affirmed the validity of culturally distinct churches for culturally distinct people.[51]

One doesn't have to look very deeply into the Acts 6:1-7 account of the distribution of food to the two different groups of widows in Jerusalem to realize that Luke is hardly telling us by this incident that one shouldn't establish a heterogeneous congregation. Nor was the purpose of the decisions of the Jerusalem Council to set up two culturally distinct churches.[52]

Even apart from other quite obvious theological deficiencies in the various statements quoted above, the contention that the early church grew when the homogeneous unit principle was followed and failed to grow when it was ignored is a conclusion that simply cannot be reached from a careful study of the book of Acts. Just the opposite, in fact, appears to be the case. One can hardly think of two more distinct groups than Jews and Gentiles. Yet, so far as we can gather from Acts and the epistles, never did Paul establish separate Jewish congregations and gentile congregations. The two were one, not just in the *Una Sancta* but in the visible groups gathered together around the means of grace.

This is not to say that at times it may not be wise to think in terms of establishing separate congregations within a community. There may be a language barrier that makes it difficult, if not impossible, for two groups to worship together; or there may be a very pronounced cultural barrier, which would make both groups feel much more at ease and comfortable worshiping with "their own kind of people." We are thinking here not only of racial but also of economic and other cultural differences. Congregations tend to develop their own personalities through a combination of things, not the least of which is the socioeconomic level of the majority of their members. People who feel at home in one congregation may not feel that way in another. When the circumstances permit it, there is certainly nothing unscriptural in having a multiplicity of congregations from which to choose.

On the world mission level, likewise, circumstances may at times dictate that work be done among a specific class of people in the recognition that in a particular society people have been conditioned for generations not to cross over certain boundaries. One has to work with the situation as it is.

But to say that the Scriptures direct us to such a pattern of mission work is entirely unwarranted. The pattern the book of Acts presents is, in fact, just the opposite. The gospel is for "all the nations," regardless of race or color, caste or class. The ideal, then, would always be to seek to plant and nurture heterogeneous congregations right from the beginning, yet without failing to recognize that different ethnic, economic, and social groups may require us to use different mission strategies if we are to effectively reach these groups with the gospel.

5. *Paul concentrated his efforts in areas where the gospel had not yet been preached.*

We do not have to spend any time developing this statement since Paul himself made it clear that this was an essential element of his mission strategy (Romans 15:20; 2 Corinthians 10:13-16), but we do well to ask what place this strategy should have in our mission strategy today.

The situation is different, of course. We are well beyond the days of the early spread of the gospel. There are very few areas left in the world that have not heard of the name of Jesus. Yet, on the other hand, there are many areas in the world today that are not being served by Christian missionaries. Quite an imbalance, in fact, exists. According to statistics from Ralph Winter's United States Center for Word Mission in Pasadena, California, 91 percent of missionaries from North America are working in areas of the world where the church has already been established and has a relatively strong presence, while only 9 percent are attempting to reach those among whom there is no, or only a minimal, Christian witness.

The statistics presented by Waldo Werning are quite similar:

About 90 percent of Christian leadership works with 10 percent of the world's population. We are told that if all Christian communities would reach effectively through evangelistic thrusts into their own communities, less than 20 percent of the world would be reached. Most non-Christians in the world have no Christian neighbors.[53]

The situation is critical, especially when we think of the vast number of people living right now, an estimated 9 percent of everyone who ever lived.[54] The majority of that number not only *is not* at the present time being served by Christian missionaries but *cannot* be since the areas in which these people live are closed to missionaries.

If, as we assume you would agree, Paul's strategy of bringing the gospel to places where others were not bringing it has relevance yet today, then it appears that we need to step up efforts at alternate ways of doing mission work. One way is through the use of radio to broadcast the gospel into otherwise inaccessible areas, something that we have barely begun to do. It appears that we should be expanding our efforts in this area.

We could also be doing more to utilize laypeople as *informal* missionaries, businessmen and technicians of various kinds, who are welcome in some places into which the missionary cannot enter. To make maximum use of such people, training courses could be designed and then offered to those who have the opportunity to freely enter nations closed to the formal spread of the gospel.

Could we not also make use of theologically trained people in this way? Could they not offer some skill they possess, or for which they have taken special training, to a nation in need of that skill and then enter that country, not as clergymen, but as teachers? They would then have a chance, on an informal basis, to give an answer to those among whom they labor regarding the hope that is in them. The present situation requires new, creative approaches to bring the old, and only, saving truth to the many who may never have the opportunity to hear it if we rely on traditional mission methodology. It strikes this essayist that if Paul, resourceful man that he was, were living today, he would be exploring every possible vehicle for the spread of the gospel to those who haven't heard it.

The need for such resourcefulness applies equally to the home front. Although no legal barriers in our nation prevent Christians from evangelizing the unchurched, other kinds of barriers may make it extremely difficult to reach certain groups, for example, those who are turned off by the "institutional church," the intellectuals, the apartment dwellers, the very poor, and those of a different race or culture. If traditional evangelistic approaches seem to be ineffective, then let other ways be tried. It is the message that is timeless and must not be changed; but the methods, the ways by which Christians bring the message to others, are not timeless. Methods can and should change according to the times and circumstances as we seek to be all things to all men that by all possible means we might win some.

1. Which three men were on the missionary team that set out from Antioch? *Paul, Barnabas, Mark*

2. Who led the church in Antioch to commission these men? *Holy Spirit*

3. Trace Paul's first missionary journey on a map. (Rather than using a map that already has his journeys traced, find a blank map of Asia Minor and Greece, put in the appropriate cities if needed, and draw your own lines.) What are the key events that happened in each of these locations?

   - Cyprus *Sergius Paulus is amazed at word, sorcerer Elymas blind from word*

   - Antioch of Pisidia *church established, word being carried*

   - Iconium *Jews & Gentiles believed, spoke boldly for Lord (P&B)*

   - Lystra *Paul stoned + left for dead, preaches in open air*

   - Derbe *large # of disciples*

4. What did Paul do after he completed his work in Derbe? *returned to Antioch + reported what God did through him*

5. What doctrinal error was corrected by the council in Jerusalem (see Acts 15:1-35)? Why was a favorable decision on the part of the council vital if Paul was to continue his missionary work? *- circumcised or not -showed he could preach to Gentiles*

6. Over what did Barnabas and Paul disagree as they were about to begin their second missionary journey? Who do you think was right? *- take Mark or not - Paul*

7. Trace Paul's second missionary journey on a map. What are the key events that happened in each of these locations?

   - Lystra *picked up Timothy*

   - Western Asia Minor (as Paul and his team were trying to decide where God wanted them to work) *God did not allow*

   - Troas *Luke, Macedonia call for help*

   - Philippi *baptizing jailer + family, anti-semitic*

   - Thessalonica *converted heathens*

   - Berea *escorted out for safety*

   - Athens *witnessed in marketplace*

Priscilla & Aquilla

- Corinth *religio licta, long stay - gospel spreads past Corinth*
- (Return to Antioch) *takes time off after visiting Jerusalem*

8. In what city did Paul spend most of the time on his second missionary journey? What were some of the things that happened in this city? *Corinth ↑*

9. Trace Paul's third missionary journey on a map. Much of his time was spent in Ephesus. That will be the first city on your map. Then, using Acts 20:1-6, follow his route as he revisited the cities he started on his second journey. Be sure to trace his journey to its end point.

10. Give at least one example of how Paul put the following principles into practice during his missionary travels:

- He was open to the leading of the Lord.
  Asia Minor (God intervened)
- He viewed opposition and setbacks as opportunities, not obstacles. *preached while waiting for L, T, & S*

- He carried on his work, for the most part, in key cities of the area. *Athens, Corinth*

- He started with the nucleus God provided.
  synagogues
- He established churches made up of people from a variety of backgrounds. *Thess, —heathens, Greeks, Jews*

- He concentrated his efforts in areas where the gospel had not yet been preached. *Thessalonica*

- He put no stumbling block before people other than the stumbling block of the gospel itself.
  no circumcision
- He was dedicated to team ministry.
  waited for L, T, & S

  *Priscilla
  &
  Aquilla*

Part Four _____

Paul's Mission Message

One basic message

IT IS NOT DIFFICULT to discern a common thread that is woven into the fabric of all of Paul's mission messages. Already at the time of his conversion, the risen Lord had made it clear that Paul would bring one basic message to Jew and Gentile alike. He told Ananias, "This man is my chosen instrument to *carry my name* before the Gentiles and their kings and before the people of Israel" (Acts 9:15, italics added). He told Paul directly, "I am sending you to them [to the Jews and to the Gentiles] to open their eyes and turn them from darkness to light, and from the power of Satan to God, so that they may receive forgiveness of sins and a place among those who are sanctified by faith in me" (Acts 26:17,18).

Paul accomplished this by preaching Jesus, crucified and risen. Through Jesus and through him alone was rescue from Satan to be found, as well as forgiveness of sins and a place in the family of God. Paul's message was centered on the cross and the empty tomb.

We don't have to spend much time demonstrating that Paul did just that. He told the Corinthians that Christ had sent him "to preach the gospel" (see 1 Corinthians 1:17), which he described as "the message of the cross" (1 Corinthians 1:18). "We preach Christ crucified," he emphasized (1 Corinthians 1:23). "When I came to you, brothers," he wrote, "I did not come with eloquence or superior wisdom as I proclaimed to you the testimony about God. For I resolved to know nothing while I was with you except Jesus Christ and him crucified" (1 Corinthians 2:1,2). "I want to remind you of the gospel I preached to you," he told them, and then he went on to describe that gospel: "Christ died for our sins according to the Scriptures, . . . he was buried, . . . he was raised on the third day according to the Scriptures" (1 Corinthians 15:1,3,4). This was, as he put it, a message of "first importance" (1 Corinthians 15:3).

It wasn't just in Corinth that he preached that message. To the Galatians he wrote, "Before your very eyes Jesus Christ was clearly portrayed as crucified" (Galatians 3:1). In the synagogue of Antioch of Pisidia, he preached about the death and resurrection of Jesus through whom alone there is forgiveness of sins (Acts 13:28-37). In Thessalonica, also in the synagogue, "on three Sabbath days he reasoned with them from the Scriptures, explaining and proving that the Christ had to suffer and rise from the dead" (Acts 17:2,3). In Athens, both in the Agora and before the Council of the Areopagus, he preached "the good news about Jesus and the resurrection" (Acts 17:18). In Ephesus, "he told the people to believe in the one coming after him [John the Baptist], that is, in Jesus" (Acts 19:4).

Paul put first things first. He first established the foundation and then built upon that foundation. And the foundation was always the same wherever he went and whatever people he worked among; for, as he told the Corinthians, "no one can lay any foundation other than the one already laid, which is Jesus Christ" (1 Corinthians 3:11). There cannot be more than one gospel. Any other "gospel" than the good news of forgiveness of sins through Jesus, crucified and risen, is, as he told the Galatians, "really no gospel at all" (Galatians 1:7).

Here is perhaps the place to mention briefly a "gospel substitute" that has made quite a bit of headway in our day, the so-called liberation gospel. The liberation gospel, or theology of liberation, goes beyond the social gospel (which also continues to have its proponents) in that it argues that "the church must become actively engaged in helping to revolutionize society, getting rid of the oppressors and the causes of oppression."[55]

E. H. Wendland, in an essay entitled "An Evaluation of Current Missiology," points clearly to the weakness of such a "gospel":

> It should be quite clear from Scripture that the theology of liberation with its almost total emphasis upon the things of this world makes a mockery of the Christian's real spiritual assurance which rests in the Savior's promise of the forgiveness of sin and the hope of everlasting life. One critic, J. D. Gort, has called it a "kind of liberation which is undistinguishable from what is offered by the politician, philosopher, physician, social worker, psychiatrist and economist" and which leads to "a new enslavement." One would certainly hesitate to preach a "gospel of liberation" to a conscience troubled by sin or to a person who cries to God for help at the graveside of a loved one.
>
> Our own Synod's statement *This We Believe* says it well: "We reject . . . all attempts to interpret eschatological passages in the New Testament . . . symbolically, or see these eschatological events taking place not in the end of time, but concurrently with history." As Christians our final goal is to be found in a new heaven and a new earth, to be consummated when the Lord Jesus comes again.[56]

Paul likewise had no use for a social gospel or a liberation gospel. Though "the whole fabric of society in the cities of the Empire was built upon slavery,"[57] we do not find so much as one word or even a veiled hint in Acts or Paul's epistles that the business of the church was to eradicate slavery. Nothing but Christ crucified and risen; that was Paul's message.

Different approaches

But as similar as Paul's basic mission message was as he traveled from place to place, his was very far from a "canned speech" approach. He communicated the one message in a manner relevant to each situation. Edgar Hoenecke says it well when he speaks of "the complete freedom from hidebound rules in St. Paul's approach and his remarkable flexibility in adapting himself and his message to all sorts of people and situations." Paul, he writes, "is the greatest exponent and teacher of Christian doctrine after Christ, and yet one will search in vain for a set pattern of dialectic preaching or teaching in his sermons."[58]

The three mission messages of Paul that Luke has preserved, at least in summary form, bear this out. They are preached in three dissimilar situations to three dissimilar audiences and serve as a fine example of what Paul means when he says, "I have become all things to all men so that by all possible means I might save some" (1 Corinthians 9:22).

1. *Antioch of Pisidia (Acts 13:16-41)*

The first is his sermon in the synagogue at Antioch of Pisidia on the first journey. A typical synagogue service began with a recitation of the *Shema* (Deuteronomy 6:4-9), followed by the prayers. Then would come two readings, one from the law and the other from the prophets. The prayers were sometimes said in the vernacular; the Scriptures, however, were always read first in Hebrew and then, if necessary, in the Greek of the Septuagint or in a paraphrase of the spoken language of the country.[59]

This would be followed by an address, often, as here, called a message of encouragement, which could be given by any competent Jew in attendance. Paul responded to the invitation of the synagogue rulers to offer such a message of encouragement with an address heavily laced with Old Testament references. Such an approach was only logical, since the audience here, of course, was somewhat to very knowledgeable of the Old Testament.

Paul began by briefly summarizing Old Testament history from Abraham to David (verses 16-22) to make it clear that he was not preaching a new religion. Then he proceeded from David to the Savior, Jesus, descended from David as promised by God and as testified to by John the Baptist. Paul spoke of John the Baptist without any word of explanation. The message of John the Baptist seems to have been known by members of the synagogues in Asia Minor. At least this was the situation in Ephesus (see Acts 18:24-26; 19:1-3). In this way Paul demonstrated once again that the message he was preaching did not contradict but fulfilled the Old Testament (verses 23-25). Third, Paul showed that what happened to Jesus in Jerusalem, both his death at the hands of the people and their rulers and his resurrection, fulfilled the Scriptures (verses 26-37). Paul concluded with an announcement of forgiveness and justification through Jesus, a justification "from everything you could not be justified from by the law of Moses," as well as a warning not to take this message lightly (verses 38-41).

It is possible that Luke intended this relatively lengthy message to serve as an example of all of Paul's initial sermons in the synagogues he visited. Compare this sermon with the brief résumé Luke gives us of Paul's message in the synagogue at Thessalonica: "On three Sabbath days he reasoned with them from the Scriptures, explaining and proving that the Christ had to suffer and rise from the dead. 'This Jesus I am proclaiming to you is the Christ,' he said" (Acts 17:2,3). Paul's point of contact was what he and the synagogue worshipers had in common: the Old Testament Scriptures. From that common starting ground, Paul proceeded to his message: the heart and center of the Scriptures, Jesus Christ, crucified and risen, through whom alone there is forgiveness and justification.

2. Lystra (Acts 14:15-17)

At Lystra the audience was considerably different. Though, as a Roman colony, it had been inhabited by a considerable number of Roman soldiers, active or retired, it does not appear that Romans, or at least any sizable number of them, were in Paul's audience. And even though Timothy, a half-Jew, was apparently from Lystra, it does not appear that Jews were a major part of his audience either. His audience, rather, consisted largely of uneducated, unsophisticated Lycaonians.

Paul's address in Lystra, then, is an example of the way he brought the Word to untutored pagans. It was precipitated by Paul's healing of a lame man, which led the people to conclude that Paul and Barnabas were the gods Hermes and Zeus. ("Two inscriptions discovered at Sedasa, near Lystra, dating from the middle of the third century A.D., identify the Greek gods Zeus and Hermes as being worshiped in Lycaonian Galatia.")[60]

It is quite possible that the people were acquainted with the ancient legend of Philemon and Baucis, which was well known in southern Galatia.[61] According to this legend, Zeus and Hermes, disguised as mortals, once came to the Phrygian hill country seeking lodging. They asked at a thousand homes, and no one took them in. Finally a very poor couple, Philemon and Baucis, did welcome them and gave them a sumptuous meal that almost depleted their meager resources. In appreciation Zeus and Hermes transformed their cottage of straw and reeds into a temple with a golden roof and marble columns, and they appointed Philemon and Baucis as priest and priestess of the temple. As for the inhospitable people, Zeus and Hermes destroyed their homes.

It could well be that, seeing the healing of the crippled man and remembering the legend, the people didn't want to make the same mistake twice and ignore the gods when they appeared. Rather, they determined to offer sacrifice to them, an act that Paul and Barnabas emotionally protested by tearing their clothes.

In his response Paul did not begin with the revealed knowledge of God in the Scriptures but with natural knowledge. He asserted that he and Barnabas were not gods but were human beings who had come to bring the Lystrans good news about the living God. Paul then pointed the Lystrans to God as the Creator, "the living God, who made heaven and earth and sea and everything in them," and to God as preserver, "He has shown kindness by giving you rain from heaven and crops in their seasons; he provides you with plenty of food and fills your hearts with joy." Paul called them to "turn from these worthless things" (that is, worship of the creature rather than the Creator) to the worship of the one true God.

In his message at Lystra, Paul didn't talk about Jesus and his death and resurrection at all; but this was undoubtedly because the people, in their desire to offer sacrifices to Paul and Barnabas, didn't allow Paul to finish his message. What we have here, then, is an approach to evangelism, preevangelism, if you will, which would have led, if the occasion had permitted, into the greater things the one true God had done for the Lystrans and all people.

3. *Athens (Acts 17:22-31)*

Labeling Paul a "babbler"[62] (Acts 17:18), the Epicurean and Stoic philosophers brought Paul to a meeting of the Areopagus so that his teaching could be formally examined. As Paul stood before this council, he didn't quote the Jewish Scriptures as at Antioch,[63] nor did he develop his argument from the God who gives rain and crops in their season as at Lystra. His point of contact, rather, was the altar he had seen with the inscription "TO AN UNKNOWN GOD."[64] "What you worship as something unknown," he tells them, "I am going to proclaim to you" (verses 22,23).

In the course of his address in which he tells the Athenians who the Unknown God is (verses 24-29), Paul demonstrates the folly of idolatry and also skillfully puts down both the deism of the Epicureans and the pantheism of the Stoics.

God is not to be pantheistically equated with the world, for God "*made* the world and everything in it."

God is over and above the world and therefore cannot possibly "live in temples built by hands,"[65] nor can he, the Creator of man, be diminished to "an image made by man's design and skill" from things like gold or silver or stone.

Yet though the God who made the world is over and above the world, he did not adopt a hands-off policy, as deistic philosophy asserts. On the contrary, "he himself gives all men life and breath and *everything else*." "He determined the times set for [people] and the exact places where they should live." And his purpose in doing this was "so that men would seek him and perhaps reach out for him and find him." Far from wanting to be aloof from his creation, God desired fellowship with it.

Paul uses excerpts from two Greek poems to back up his contention that God is both the Creator and thus separate from, and the preserver and thus deeply concerned about, his creation: "In him we live and move and have our being" (Epimenides, around 600 B.C.) and "We are his offspring" (Aratus, around 315–240 B.C.).[66] Both poems are in honor of Zeus. Obviously, as Longenecker puts it:

> By such maxims Paul is not suggesting that God is to be thought of in terms of the Zeus of Greek polytheism or Stoic pantheism.

He is rather arguing that the poets his hearers recognized as authorities have to some extent corroborated his message. In his search for a measure of common ground with his hearers, he is, so to speak, disinfecting and rebaptizing the poet's words for his own purposes.[67]

Having made clear who the Unknown God is, Paul concludes with a call to repentance:

In the past God overlooked such ignorance [that is, worshiping created images rather than the Creator], but now he commands all people everywhere to repent. For he has set a day when he will judge the world with justice by the man he has appointed. He has given proof of this to all men by raising him from the dead. (verses 30,31)

Did Paul know that when he spoke these words before the Areopagus he was directly contradicting the Athenian tragedian Aeschylus? About 500 years before that day, when describing the institution of the Areopagus by Athene, the city's patron deity, Aeschylus put these words into the mouth of the god Apollo:

When the dust has soaked up a man's blood,
Once he is dead, there is no resurrection.[68]

It would have been easier, of course, for Paul simply to have affirmed the immortality of the soul. That the Greeks, at least many of them, could readily have accepted. But Paul's purpose was not to please but to proclaim the truth.

Key characteristics of Paul's mission message

1. *Paul's message was contextual and conciliatory but not compromising.*

His message was contextual, that is, it was related to the cultural context of the society in which it was proclaimed, and it was nonpolemical in tone. He did not set out to alienate his audience but to woo and win it. But though his message was contextual and conciliatory, it was never compromising. Roland Allen compares the uncompromising nature of Paul's missionary message with the weak, anemic mission philosophy of his day, a philosophy not unknown today, which saw as the missionary's task "not to call men from the heathen temple into the Church of God but to trim the dimly glowing lamp of God in the heathen temple, and to pour into it a few drops of the oil of Christian doctrine till it shines with a new radiance."[69] In Paul's message, Allen correctly asserts:

> There was no weak condoning of the offense of idolatry, no eager anxiety to make the best of a false religion, no hazy suggestion that every religion, if only it is rightly understood, is a worship of the true God and a teaching which leads to Him. St. Paul gave his hearers a perfectly clear, definite understanding of what was required of them. To enjoy the hope set before them they must be prepared for a complete break with the past. . . . There was no easy road to Christ's glory, no making the best of both worlds, no hope of salvation but in Christ.[70]

In all three of his mission messages, Paul refuses to compromise. He tells those in the synagogue at Antioch, "Through him [Jesus] everyone who believes is justified from everything you could not be justified from by the law of Moses" (Acts 13:39). In Lystra (Acts 14:15), Paul calls the practice of idolatry *worthless*. The Greek means "vain" or "futile" (see 1 Corinthians 15:17). Paul therefore urges the Lystrans to turn away from it. In Athens, he ends his message on the one truth he knew the council of the Areopagus would have the most difficulty accepting, the resurrection. He was uncompromising, since only the truth sets people free (John 8:32).

There are boundaries, then, beyond which one will not go if he is determined to be a faithful transmitter of the gospel. But this does not mean that, within proper bounds, one won't seek to tailor his message to the audience.

E. H. Wendland, in the essay cited previously, "An Evaluation of Current Missiology," applies this truth to the world mission field:

> When, for example, an American is doing mission work in Africa, he should be aware that he is working among people who think in different patterns, speak in a different language, and express themselves in other ways. People coming to Christ should not be made to feel that he is a "foreign" Christ. Neither should they worship in situations which reflect an entirely foreign culture. "The gospel in context," as someone has expressed it succinctly, "brings Christ as both Savior and Brother."[71]

But, at the same time, Wendland sounds the same caution we have voiced earlier: "Where native custom and culture come into conflict with the teachings of Scripture, we'll not be afraid to proclaim the truth no matter how disturbing this might be to cultural sensitivities."[77] Sensitivity to the truth and to the situation of the people to whom we want to bring the truth—when both of these factors are present, our approach will be contextual and conciliatory and yet will not compromise the message.

2. *His message was persuasive but not dependent on the power of human logic.*

Paul knew quite well that he had no power to convert anyone. He realized that the power of sin and Satan over people was greater than his power to overcome these enemies. He knew that human beings weren't born with a little spark of the divine in them which he simply had to fan into a flame. The fact is that the people to whom he came were dead, "dead in . . . transgressions and sins" (Ephesians 2:1). He couldn't raise a dead person.

Only the Holy Spirit can quicken a dead heart and lead it to call Jesus Lord (1 Corinthians 12:3); and the Spirit accomplishes this miracle through the gospel—"the power of God for the salvation of everyone who believes" (Romans 1:16). "Eloquence" or "superior wisdom" (1 Corinthians 2:1) on the part of the speaker cannot give the gospel a boost, nor can "wise and persuasive words" (1 Corinthians 2:4). It is the "Spirit's power" (1 Corinthians 2:4) through the gospel, not Paul's or any person's persuasiveness, that works the mighty work of faith.

Yet, at the same time, Luke used a number of verbs to demonstrate that when Paul proclaimed the Word, both in the synagogue and in the community, he did so in a very persuasive manner. Several times he used the Greek word meaning "to discuss, argue, or dispute," usually translated in the NIV as "to reason." In Thessalonica, Paul "reasoned with them [Jews and Gentiles in the synagogue] from the Scriptures, explaining [literally "opening up, expounding"] and proving [literally "setting alongside, explaining"] that the Christ had to suffer and rise from the dead" (Acts 17:2,3). In Athens he "reasoned in the synagogue with the Jews and the God-fearing Greeks, as well as in the marketplace day by day with those who happened to be there" (Acts 17:17). In Corinth "every Sabbath he reasoned in the synagogue" (Acts 18:4). In Ephesus, at the end of his second journey, he "went into the synagogue and reasoned with the Jews" (Acts 18:19). Upon his return to Ephesus on his third journey, he "entered the synagogue and spoke boldly there for three months, arguing persuasively about the kingdom of God" (Acts 19:8). When he was put out of the synagogue, "he took the disciples with him and had discussions daily in the lecture hall of Tyrannus" (Acts 19:9). Before Felix, Paul "discoursed on righteousness, self-control and the judgment to come" (Acts 24:25).

Luke used the word *persuade*. One such use was mentioned previously (Acts 19:8). It is also used in 18:4 of Paul in the synagogue at Corinth "trying *to persuade* Jews and Greeks."

In Acts 9:22, shortly after Paul's conversion, Luke used a word that literally means "to join together."[73] "Saul grew more and more powerful and baffled the Jews living in Damascus by *proving* [literally "joining together"] that Jesus is the Christ." Three years later, when Paul went up to Jerusalem for the first time, "he talked and *debated* [literally "to seek or examine together" or "to discuss or dispute"] with the Grecian Jews" (Acts 9:29).

It wasn't just Paul who handled the Word in this way. We are told that when Apollos went to Corinth, "he *vigorously refuted* [literally "to refute thoroughly"] the Jews in public debate, *proving* from the Scriptures that Jesus was the Christ" (Acts 18:28).

Why did Luke use such words when, he as well as Paul, knew that it is not the skill of the speaker but only the power of the Holy Spirit that can demonstrate, persuade, prove to people that Jesus is the Christ? There is no contradiction here at all. Paul had utmost confidence in the power of the Word, and it is precisely this confidence in the Word that led him to preach and teach it in such an unashamed, bold, confident, persuasive, and forceful manner. He knew that he was handling the *power of God*. He expected results since God himself had promised them (Isaiah 55:11).

We can do the same. Whether it be out in the world mission field, in a home mission congregation, or in a long-established congregation, whether the message is being proclaimed to one or to a multitude, whether the recipient is a believer or an unbeliever, we can, with Paul, be positive, optimistic, and confident in our proclamation. With Paul, we can put our whole heart and all our being into it because we know it will be effective. We don't have to rely on any gimmicks. Paul didn't. Just the Word, that's all we need. Through its powerful message, God accomplishes his gracious purpose.

3. His message was accompanied by signs and wonders but was not dependent on them.

A look at the place of signs and wonders in the ministry of the gospel is especially pertinent to our times. John Wimber asserts that there is a close relationship between signs and wonders and the growth of the New Testament church. "The church grew," he says, "whenever the gospel was preached, and signs and wonders followed."[74] He uses Paul's ministry at Corinth to illustrate his point:

> Perhaps the activity best suited to the use of [extraordinary] spiritual gifts is the area of evangelism. This was Paul's testimony to the Corinthians concerning his initial efforts in their lives: "My message and my preaching were not with wise and persuasive words, but with a demonstration of the Spirit's power" (1 Corinthians 2:4). In Athens, he had used persuasive words with meager results. At his next apostolic stop, Corinth, many believed. It appears that in Corinth Paul combined proclamation with demonstration, as Christ had done throughout his ministry. . . . I call this type of ministry that Paul had in Corinth power evangelism. . . . The explanation of the gospel comes with a demonstration of God's power through signs and wonders. . . . In order to see God's church multiply as it is doing in the rest of the world, the Western church must become involved in power evangelism.[75]

Our purpose here is not to enter upon a discussion of the whole charismatic movement. That, obviously, is a subject in itself.[76] But what we do want to do is examine the contention of men like Wimber that so-called power evangelism, that is, preaching combined with signs and wonders, rather than preaching alone, is what made the New Testament church grow and that such power evangelism is the means by which the Holy Spirit will cause the church to grow today. We will narrow that down even further by looking at the connection between Paul's preaching and the signs and wonders that he performed.

Luke, in his account of Paul's missionary journeys, recorded six occasions when Paul performed signs and wonders.

1. (Acts 13:7-12) In Paphos on the island of Cyprus, Sergius Paulus "sent for Barnabas and Saul because he wanted to hear the word of God." Elymas "tried to turn the proconsul from the faith." Paul, "filled with the Holy Spirit," struck Elymas blind. "When the proconsul saw what had happened, he believed, for he was amazed at the teaching about the Lord."

2. (Acts 14:1-3) In Iconium, Paul and Barnabas entered the synagogue and "spoke so effectively that a great number of Jews and Gentiles believed." He remained there for a time, "speaking boldly for the Lord, who confirmed the message of his grace by enabling them to do miraculous signs and wonders."

3. (Acts 14:8-18) In Lystra, he healed the man lame from birth. The result was that the people began to worship Paul and Barnabas as gods and in their desire to offer sacrifice to them apparently didn't let Paul finish his message.

4. (Acts 16:32,33) In Philippi, Paul drove an evil spirit out of a slave girl, for which he and Silas were beaten and imprisoned. Following an earthquake, Paul and Silas "spoke the word of the Lord to him [the jailer] and to all the others in his house . . . and he and all his family were baptized."

5. (Acts 19:8-12,18-20) In Ephesus, "Paul entered the synagogue and spoke boldly there for three months, arguing persuasively about the kingdom of God." This was followed by two years of daily discussions in the lecture hall of Tyrannus, "so that all the Jews and Greeks who lived in the province of Asia heard the word of the Lord. God did extraordinary miracles through Paul, so that even handkerchiefs and aprons that had touched him were taken to the sick, and their illnesses were cured and the evil spirits left them." Toward the end of Paul's stay in Ephesus, "many of those who believed now came and openly confessed their evil deeds. A number who had practiced sorcery brought their scrolls together and burned them publicly. . . . In this way [that is, as unbelievers saw believers' faith in action] the word of the Lord spread widely and grew in power."

6. (Acts 20:9,10) In Troas, while engaged in speaking to a group of fellow believers, Paul raised Eutychus from the dead.

Luke did not record any miracles performed in Corinth, but Paul, writing to the Corinthians, said, "The things that mark an apostle—signs, wonders and miracles—were done among you with great perseverance" (2 Corinthians 12:12).

There is no mention of signs and wonders being performed in any of the other places in which we have a record of Paul proclaiming the Word: Damascus, Jerusalem, Antioch of Syria, Salamis, Antioch of Pisidia, Derbe, Perga, Thessalonica, Berea, Athens, and Rome. An argument from silence is not conclusive, of course. Paul certainly may have performed more miracles than Luke recorded. What is instructive is that, as Ramsay puts it, "the marvels recorded in Acts are not, as a rule, said to have been efficacious in spreading the new religion."[77]

Of the miracles of Paul, only one, striking Elymas blind at Paphos, could possibly be construed as leading a person to faith. But even here, as we brought out earlier, it wasn't the miracle that converted Sergius Paulus. Luke connected his coming to faith with "the teaching about the Lord" (Acts 13:12).

The truth of the matter is that all the examples drawn from Paul's ministry are fully in line with such normative statements as Romans 10:13-17:

> "Everyone who calls on the name of the Lord will be saved."
> How, then, can they call on the one they have not believed in? And how can they believe in the one of whom they have not heard? And how can they hear without someone preaching to them?
> . . . Consequently, faith comes from hearing the message, and the message is heard through the word of Christ.

The failure of Wimber and others in the Church Growth Movement and the Pentecostal/charismatic camp to recognize this stems from their failure to recognize and appreciate the power that the gospel has in and of itself. Note how Wimber separates God's power from the gospel: "The explanation of the gospel comes with a demonstration of God's power through signs and wonders." The gospel, according to Wimber, apparently is something that is simply *explained*, something that human logic can chew on and make a rational decision about, while signs and wonders display God's power and thus move one to make a favorable decision about the gospel.

A denial of the inherent power of the gospel leads one to look elsewhere for power. Paul, on the other hand, saw that the real power lay in the gospel itself. *"It is the power of God for salvation"* (Romans 1:16, italics added). The difference between Paul's reception at Athens and at Corinth did not lie in the fact that in Athens Paul relied on human persuasion and in Corinth on Spirit-wrought signs and wonders. The message was the same in both places, but in Athens the seed fell for the most part on the beaten path as the Athenians exercised their prerogative to reject the message that had the power to save them.

What purpose, then, did signs and wonders serve in the ministry of Paul? Three purposes come to mind:

1. Paul's signs and wonders helped to authenticate him and his message. These were "things that mark an apostle" (2 Corinthians 12:12). For example, Paul used the "miraculous signs and wonders God had done among the Gentiles" (Acts 15:12) through himself and Barnabas as a way of demonstrating to the Jews in Jerusalem that his gospel was the same divinely given message as theirs.

2. Paul's signs and wonders at times served the purpose of attracting hearers, thus preparing the way for preaching (see Lystra). The same thing happened when Peter and John healed the lame man (see Acts 3:11,12).

3. Paul's signs and wonders were "illustrations of the character of the new religion."[78] People would be led to see that Christianity was a religion of love. Heathen magicians and exorcists would heal to line their pockets. Paul did so out of love.

Should we expect signs and wonders yet today? In The People's Bible commentary *1 Corinthians*, Carleton Toppe gives a careful answer, one which this writer endorses:

> As far as "gifts of healing" and "miraculous powers" are concerned, these gifts were granted to believers only when and where the Spirit willed, even in the days of the apostles. Certainly God has always been able to perform miracles of healing through whom he wills, but it is another matter for an individual Christian to prove that he or she has that power today. Many so-called miracles are counterfeit. Sober-minded Christians also

question whether miracles of healing are as necessary today as they were when they served a special purpose in the early days of the Christian church. Furthermore, they recognize that the great works of spiritual healing God is constantly accomplishing are far more vital than the miraculous physical healing that charismatics profess they can perform.[79]

To accomplish these great works of spiritual healing, one must do battle with the powerful "spiritual forces of evil in the heavenly realms" (Ephesians 6:12). Only the more powerful Word of the gospel will be able to win that victory (Ephesians 6:13-17). Works of physical help serve, as they did with Paul, only the subsidiary purpose of attracting hearers and demonstrating the love of our Savior, a love that his followers seek to emulate.

1. What message had the Lord called Paul to preach? See Acts 9:15 and Acts 26:17,18. *Jesus was crucified for our sins + has risen*

2. How did Paul follow God's call in . . .

   - Corinth? (1 Corinthians 1:23; 2:1,2; 15:1-4) *preached of crucifixion + resurrection w/ first importance*
   - Galatia? (Galatians 3:1) *preached about crucifixion giving forgiveness*
   - Thessalonica? (Acts 17:2,3) *explained (3 Sabbaths) how Christ had to suffer + rise*
   - Athens? (Acts 17:17,18) *good news about Jesus + resurrection (in agora)*
   - Ephesus? (Acts 19:4) *believe in Jesus*

3. Why is it vital to include the resurrection when talking about Jesus and his work? *Shows that Jesus is God*

4. Compare three of Paul's presentations of the gospel. Luke records his sermons in . . .

   - Antioch in Pisidia. (Acts 13:16-41) *many OT references, showed how it fulfilled scriptures*

   - Lystra. (Acts 14:15-17) *natural knowledge, preevangelism*

   - Athens. (Acts 17:22-31) *talks of Unknown God, backs up w/ Greek poems*

   Read these sermons and, as you do, answer the following questions:

   - What was the makeup of his audience? *some Jews + more Gentiles*

   - How did he lead up to the gospel message? *by giving them background knowledge for their culture*
   - What sources did he quote? *sources they would know*
   - What was the conclusion of each of the sermons? *call to repentance . . .*
   - How did Paul fit his message to his audience? *changed it according to culture*

5. Evaluate this statement of E. H. Wendland:

   When, for example, an American is doing mission work in Africa, he should be aware that he is working among people who think in different patterns, speak in a different language, and express themselves in other ways. People coming to Christ should not be made to feel that he is a "foreign" Christ. Neither should they worship in situations which reflect an entirely foreign culture. "The gospel in context," as someone has expressed it succinctly, "brings Christ as both Savior and Brother."

   nicely said, we want people to believe God is their God + everyone's God, not just an American God

Study Questions

6. What message did Paul always proclaim, even though some of the people turned away when they heard it?

   the truth — *there is only one true God, + faith alone in him saves*

7. How important is it for Christians to speak logically, persuasively, and passionately when sharing their faith with others?

   we know God's Word will work

8. What role does reason play in a person's presenting the gospel message to another person? What role can reason not play?

   help show God — *not understand God or come to salvation*

9. Luke mentions six places where Paul performed signs and wonders (Paphos, Iconium, Lystra, Philippi, Ephesus, and Troas). What role did signs and wonders have in Paul's ministry? Note the following passages:

   - John 13:35 *know that Paul is sent from God*

   - Romans 10:13-17 *they can call on God because they "heard" him*

   - Acts 14:8-11 *shows God has power, opens doors for witnessing about true God*

   - 2 Corinthians 12:12; Acts 15:12

   shows apostleship, people will listen

10. What place do food pantries, medical care, and other forms of humanitarian assistance have in the church's ministry?

    they help open doors for evangelism

Part Five

Paul's Follow-Up

IN THIS FINAL PART OF OUR STUDY of Paul's mission message and methodology, we want to look at two main aspects of Paul's follow-up strategy. We will note that he nurtured those he had evangelized and that he established indigenous churches.

Paul nurtured those he had evangelized

He did this in a number of ways:

1. *Already on his first visit, he sought to build upon the basic gospel message.*

In many cases this was not possible, at least to any great degree, since more often than not he wasn't permitted to remain in a place for any great length of time. But when he did have that opportunity, he went far beyond the basics. As a result of his stay of three years in Ephesus, for example, he was able to tell the elders of that congregation: "I have not hesitated to proclaim to you the whole will of God" (Acts 20:27). He didn't leave anything out. His goal was, as he told the Colossians, to "present everyone perfect [literally "complete"] in Christ" (Colossians 1:28).

> Even when he did not have such a lengthy period of time at a place, Paul crammed as much teaching as he possibly could into the number of days the Lord gave him. He fed the people, even brand-new believers, meat as well as milk. Though he may have spent as few as three weeks in Thessalonica, during that brief time he managed to find time to teach them not just the basic message of sin and grace, but even the doctrine of the Antichrist (2 Thessalonians 2).[80]

2. *He revisited personally the churches he founded, in order to strengthen the believers in their faith.*

On the first journey, having reached the city of Derbe in the region of Lycaonia, Paul and Barnabas turned around and retraced their steps: "They returned to Lystra, Iconium and Antioch, strengthening the disciples and encouraging them to remain true to the faith. 'We must go through many hardships to enter the kingdom of God,' they said" (Acts 14:21,22). Their work of "strengthening the disciples" most assuredly consisted of further teaching of the Word.

At the beginning of the second journey, Paul, along with Silas, "went through Syria and Cilicia, strengthening the churches" (Acts 15:41), churches probably founded sometime prior to Paul's first journey. They also revisited the churches of Galatia. As a result of this visitation, "the churches were strengthened in the faith and grew daily in numbers" (Acts 16:5).

At the start of the third journey, Paul once again "traveled from place to place throughout the region of Galatia and Phrygia,[81] strengthening all the disciples" (Acts 18:23). This made the fourth time Paul had visited the Galatian congregations. He then went to Ephesus, where he had already briefly presented the gospel on his second journey (Acts 18:19-21). Now it was time for a more in-depth presentation of the Word. At the close of the third journey, Paul revisited the churches he had founded on his second journey: He "set out for Macedonia [where he had founded congregations in Philippi, Thessalonica, and Berea]. He traveled through that area, speaking many words of encouragement to the people, and finally arrived in Greece, where he stayed three months [probably in Corinth]" (Acts 20:1-3). His entire third journey, in fact, was more nurturing than evangelistic in nature.

3. He utilized coworkers in the revisitation of churches.

Coworkers were important to Paul. On relatively few occasions do we find Paul alone. Usually it was just a temporary situation when, for one reason or another, he had left a companion or was waiting for one to join him. At Athens, for example, Paul was by himself for a time, having been brought there from Berea because of persecution, but he was soon joined by Silas and Timothy. It doesn't take much reading in the epistles of Paul to see what value these coworkers were personally to Paul. (See the long list in Romans 16; also Philippians 2:22-30 and 4:3; Colossians 4:7-15; 2 Timothy 4:11; Titus 3:12,13; and Philemon 23,24.). Paul was clearly a team player.[82] Our present world mission policy of making sure to send out more than one missionary to a field certainly has scriptural precedent. Would it be wise to do the same with new home mission starts?

Not only were these team members a blessing to Paul, however. Paul was also a blessing to them. As Paul had earlier been an apprentice under Barnabas, so, in the course of Paul's long and fruitful ministry, many were apprentices under Paul. As Jesus had called the Twelve to be with him before he sent them out to preach (see Mark 3:14), so these men were with Paul, some on a more regular basis than others, receiving from Paul a one-on-one seminary training. These men, then, Paul sent out, not only to start new missions but especially, from what we can glean from Acts and the epistles, to nurture those that had been started.

Take just one example: Timothy. On his second journey, Paul sent this young man as his emissary from Athens to Thessalonica to "strengthen and encourage" the Thessalonians in their faith, "so that no one would be unsettled" by the trials they were undergoing (1 Thessalonians 3:2,3). On his third journey, Paul dispatched Timothy from Ephesus on a difficult mission to Corinth, a congregation beset with problems (1 Corinthians 4:17; 16:10). And shortly before leaving Ephesus, Paul sent Timothy on ahead to Macedonia (Acts 19:22).

When Paul was imprisoned for the first time in Rome, he made plans to send Timothy from Rome to Philippi. He tells the Philippians: "I hope in the Lord Jesus to send Timothy to you soon. . . . I have no one else like him, who takes a genuine interest in your welfare. . . . He has served with me in the work of the gospel" (Philippians 2:19-22). Later Paul left Timothy in charge of the work in Ephesus (1 Timothy 1:3).

Paul was well aware of the devil's power, that he works on new believers both from within and from without. "I know that after I leave," Paul told the elders of the church at Ephesus, "savage wolves will come in among you and will not spare the flock. Even from your own number men will arise and distort the truth in order to draw away disciples after them. So be on your guard!" (Acts 20:29-31). That is why Paul himself, through his visits and revisits, did what he could to prepare the flocks for the overt, as well as the subtle, attacks of the old evil foe. And that is why what Paul couldn't do in person for the congregations he had founded he sought to carry out through faithful coworkers. Nurture was as important as the initial proclamation of the gospel.

4. Through his letters he nurtured the congregations he founded.

These letters, which are such a blessing to the church today, were likewise a great blessing to the congregations Paul had been privileged to found. They, no less than Paul's oral messages and those of his coworkers, were instruments of nurture. In them Paul would never fail to emphasize the doctrine upon which the church rises and falls, that of justification by God's grace through faith through the redemption that came by Christ Jesus. And then he would deal with the issues of sanctification that the particular congregation to which he was writing faced at that time.

Paul's great concern for nurturing those whom he had evangelized has a bearing on contemporary mission work both at home and abroad. Evangelism methodology that begins and ends with a onetime presentation of the basic law-gospel message may well be a tool by which the Holy Spirit brings people to faith. But there needs to be more. Follow-up nurture, which strengthens the new Christian and also equips him or her for a life of Christian service, is also a vital necessity.

The same applies to the world mission field. People who are evangelized and then too quickly left to fend for themselves tend to be easy prey for the savage wolf of false doctrine. They need to be given the opportunity to grow up in their salvation once they "have tasted that the Lord is good" (see 1 Peter 2:3), to "grow in the grace and knowledge of our Lord and Savior Jesus Christ" (2 Peter 3:18), that they might "become mature, attaining to the whole measure of the fullness of Christ" (Ephesians 4:13). No "quickie" program of evangelism will accomplish that.

We also note the value of the *printed* Word and *printed* expositions of the Word. What is in print can reach some who might not be reached by the spoken message, and what is in print can be referred to and studied over and over again. Production of the People's Bible commentaries and the People's Bible Teachings is a step in the right direction. Could we not do even more by freeing up qualified persons among us to carry out writing assignments through which God's people can be nurtured?

Paul established indigenous churches

An indigenous church is a church that is able to stand on its own two feet, a church that is self-administering, self-financing, self-disciplining, and self-propagating.[83] The whole point of Roland Allen's provocative book *Missionary Methods: St. Paul's or Ours?* is that Paul's purpose was not simply to convert individuals but to establish independent churches from which the gospel would radiate to the surrounding area. That was Paul's strategy from the outset, Allen maintains, a strategy that should be ours also from the beginning stages of a mission's existence if we expect it to achieve indigeneity. Allen writes:

> If the first converts are taught to depend upon the missionary, if all work, evangelistic, educational, social is concentrated in his hands, the infant community learns to rest passively upon the man from whom they received their first insight into the gospel. . . . A tradition very rapidly grows up that nothing can be done without the authority and guidance of the missionary. The people wait for him to move, and the longer they do so, the more incapable they become of any independent action.[84]

Paul, Allen maintains, "set up no organization intermediate between his preaching and the establishment of a fully organized indigenous church."[85] Right from the beginning, the churches Paul established were self-administering, self-financing, self-disciplining, and self-propagating.

1. An indigenous church is self-administering.

There is no doubt that the churches Paul founded became self-administering in very short order. A key reason for Paul's revisitation of these churches, in fact, in addition to that of nurturing them through the Word, was to appoint spiritual leaders. This action, of course, would aid the congregations in administering their own spiritual affairs.

At the close of the first journey, we are told that "Paul and Barnabas appointed elders for them in each church and, with prayer and fasting, committed them to the Lord, in whom they had put their trust" (Acts 14:23). When Paul wrote to the Thessalonians, there was already a recognized and active group of spiritual leaders. He urged the Thessalonian believers, "Respect those who work hard among you, who are over you in the Lord and who admonish you. Hold them in the highest regard in love because of their work" (1 Thessalonians 5:12,13). It was to the elders of the church at Ephesus that Paul spoke his farewell (Acts 20:17-38). Paul addressed the epistle to the Philippians to "all the saints in Christ Jesus at Philippi, together with the overseers and deacons" (Philippians 1:1). The word *overseers* in Greek very likely refers to the same office as that of elder (compare Titus 1:5 with Titus 1:7). Deacon appears to be the second of the two primary congregational offices (see 1 Timothy 3). Sometime following his release from prison in Rome, Paul evidently traveled to Crete with Titus and brought the gospel to the people of that island. He then left Titus behind in Crete with the instruction to "appoint elders in every town" (Titus 1:5).

From the examples given, we can safely assume that Paul made sure that such spiritual leaders were put into place in all the congregations he established. And Paul expected these leaders to lead. They, not he, were to "direct the affairs of the church" (1 Timothy 5:17). These leaders, for the most part, were chosen from the midst of the local congregation. Timothy, who was not from Ephesus but who did hold a leadership position there, apparently served in somewhat of a supervisory capacity in Paul's name, with the elders responsible for the direct leadership of the congregation.

Allen lists three negative consequences if the church is led by missionaries or even by those who are taken out of the congregation, trained elsewhere, and then sent back: (1) Men so educated are often out of touch with their own congregations. They come back, so to speak, as strangers. (2) The natural leaders of village life and natural leaders of the church are silenced. The real elders of the community are not elders in the church. (3) The natural teacher is silenced, as no opportunity is given to the church itself to find its teachers.[86]

In response to this: The problem doesn't seem so much to be sending someone away for instruction (as long as the culture in the place of instruction is not too dissimilar from the one from which the person came) as it is in not allowing the church to determine who will be sent away. That can be rectified by giving the local congregation the opportunity for input as to which persons from its midst should be trained for spiritual leadership.

Paul also permitted congregations, under their own local leaders, to develop their own structures and forms. Allen rightly argues that Paul did not demand a unity of customs in the congregations he founded and that neither should we today. Allen laments:

> If a traveler returns from visiting our Indian or Chinese Christians, the first thing that he tells us is that he was delighted to find himself worshipping in a church where the language indeed was strange and the worshippers of another color, but that in every other respect he felt quite at home. He found the same sort of ornaments, the same service, the same Prayer Book, the same hymns with which he was familiar.[87]

Our missions, both here in the United States and especially in radically different cultures around the world, do not have to become clones of the mother church. Paul, says Charles Kraft, aimed for a "dynamic equivalence" church, that is, a church "that produces the same kind of impact on the people of the society of which it is a part as the original church produced upon the hearers."[88]

A church that is self-administering is more likely to take the initiative and develop its own identity peculiar to the society and culture in which it was founded and thus be more likely to attract the interest of those living around it. Take the example referred to before: worship. Paul gives virtually no instructions to the newly formed congregations regarding forms of worship. The worship that developed in Corinth, for example, could well have been different from the worship of the Christians in Jerusalem. Though Paul had to guide this worship somewhat because of certain excesses (see 1 Corinthians 14), he did not attempt to stifle it and squeeze it into a mold of his making.

Within certain bounds, there should be freedom to innovate, both on the home and on the world mission front, freedom to utilize the best forms available from the culture or, if none exist, to create appropriate ones. E. H. Wendland concludes a brief discussion of how to handle the question of worship in the church in Africa with the words:

> Here we must marvel at the foresight of the fathers. It is as though they looked to the centuries ahead and anticipated the problem. In the Augsburg Confession they put it in these words: "It is not necessary for the true unity of the Christian church that ceremonies, instituted by men, should be observed uniformly in all places" (Article VII).[89]

We will not be in disagreement, it is quite certain, over the fact that a prime goal of mission work is to establish such self-administering, indigenous churches. On the home mission front, this is accomplished fairly easily if the mission pastor is only willing to let loose the reins as people who have the gifts to provide spiritual leadership are brought into the church. On the world mission field, though, it is another story. It is not quite so easy to determine how soon this self-administration should be granted.

The way Paul dealt with the churches he established is not quite parallel to the situation on the world mission field today. It can be safely assumed, given Paul's own injunction that an elder "must not be a recent convert" (1 Timothy 3:6), that Paul drew his first leadership from the ranks of the Jews and Gentiles of the synagogue. Even in places where there may not have been synagogues, for example, Lystra and Philippi, Paul still had the opportunity to work with people who already had an acquaintance with the Old Testament. It was much easier for Paul to choose elders almost immediately than it is for a missionary today who is working almost exclusively with people who previously have had absolutely no acquaintance with the Scriptures.[90] If Paul felt it necessary to take the time to do as much nurturing as he did, even though many in his original groups may well have been quite knowledgeable of the Scriptures, it is not unreasonable to assume the need for an even greater amount of time for nurture today.

The principle, nevertheless, remains the same: The ultimate goal of mission work is an indigenous church. An indigenous church is a self-administering church. Missionaries will strive to reach that stage as soon as possible and until that time will seek to avoid giving the impression that they are permanent fixtures without whom the mission could never grow and prosper. Paul refused to use the authority he had unless it was absolutely necessary (2 Corinthians 1:24). He accepted the church's absolution of a sinner as his absolution (2 Corinthians 2:10).

2. *An indigenous church is self-financing.*

Roland Allen devotes a whole chapter of *Missionary Methods: St. Paul's or Ours?* to the question of mission financing.[91] He presents some compelling arguments for his case. Allen makes three main points. First, Paul didn't seek financial help for himself, though he recognized he had the right to do so (2 Thessalonians 3:7-10; 2 Corinthians 11:7). He did on occasion accept gifts (2 Corinthians 11:8) but not from those to whom he was preaching. He refused to do anything which would make it appear that he had come to receive or that his object was to make money.

Our expatriate missionary practice today is somewhat the same in that our missionaries do not ask for any support for themselves from those to whom they are bringing the gospel. Others back home make it possible for them to devote their time to this work, much as the Philippians helped Paul so that he could carry on his mission work in Thessalonica (Philippians 4:16).

Second, Allen notes that Paul didn't take financial support to his converts. Every congregation was financially independent. The basic principle was: "Anyone who receives instruction in the word must share all good things with his instructor" (Galatians 6:6). The only times we are aware that funds went from one congregation to another were times of acute need, for example, the famine offering from Antioch of Syria to Jerusalem (Acts 11:27-30) and the offering from Macedonia, Asia, and Galatia to Jerusalem (2 Corinthians 8,9). A comparable situation today might be the relief offerings our synod's Committee on Relief distributes in times of natural disasters.

"That one church should depend upon another for the supply of its ordinary expenses as a Church, or even for a part of them," Allen writes, "would have seemed incredible in the Four Provinces."[92]

Obviously, a much different situation prevails today. Why is this? Allen responds:

> This habit of taking supplies with us is due chiefly to two causes: first, the amazing wealth of the church at home and the notion that reverence and devotion depend upon the use of expensive religious furniture to which our luxury has accustomed us, and second, the prevalence of the idea that the stability of the church in some way depends upon the permanence of its buildings. . . . The externals of religion precede the inculcation of its principles.[93]

Allen then lists eight reasons why mission stations should not be provided with outside funds. The two most significant are the following:[94]

1. Financial subsidy tends to pauperize the converts.

Since they can't provide what they have been led to see as essential to a mission, that is, property and buildings, they learn to become passive recipients. Allen writes: "By supplying what they cannot supply we check them in the proper impulse to supply what they can supply. Foreign subsidies produce abroad all the ill effects of endowments at home, with the additional disadvantage that they are foreign. The converts learn to rely upon them instead of making every effort to supply their own needs."[95]

2. Financial subsidy tends to maintain the unity by threats of withdrawal of financial support.

The promise or hope of financial subsidy can become an artificial means of *establishing* a fellowship that only the Holy Spirit can rightfully establish as he leads us to "agree with one another" and to be "perfectly united in mind and thought" (1 Corinthians 1:10). Likewise, the fear of the loss of subsidy can become an artificial means of *preserving* that fellowship, a fellowship that "will fail," writes Allen, "the moment that any other and stronger motive urges in the direction of separation,"[96] that is, greener pastures elsewhere. That this is more than a hypothetical problem is open knowledge to anyone involved in the administration of a world mission field.

Allen also points out that Paul observed the principle that every church should administer its own funds. The reason we have trouble following that principle today is the large output of funds from the outside for which the missionary is accountable. If all funds come from the nationals, then it is natural that they would handle them also.

We do not presume to have all the answers to the questions pertaining to the financing of a mission field. Both from Paul's example and from the argumentation Allen presents, it does appear wise that our mission money is best expended by using it exclusively, or nearly so, to support the expatriate missionaries. The goal is to get expatriate missionaries in and out of one mission field and on to another as soon as possible.

We might want to think somewhat along the same lines in our home mission work. Perhaps a certain amount of start-up money could simply be given to a solid nucleus, which, after a certain period of time, would no longer be dependent on the synod, either for subsidy or for further funding. In that way our home missions could also become self-financing more quickly.

3. *An indigenous church is self-disciplining.*

If the term *self-administering* were understood as properly administering not only the physical affairs of the church but also and especially its spiritual affairs, then we would not have to list self-disciplining as a separate mark of an indigenous church.

Some who write on indigeneity, however, pass over quite lightly the need for sound, thorough indoctrination in the Word so that a church can then on its own properly administer also its spiritual affairs, as Paul certainly expected the congregations he founded to do.

Roland Allen, for example, drastically underestimates the amount of instruction that Paul gave to his converts. Allen writes: "Paul seems to have left his newly found churches with a simple system of gospel teaching, two sacraments, a tradition of the main facts of the death and resurrection, and the Old Testament."[97] A careful reading of Acts and the epistles, however, reveals that Paul taught more than the basics. In *each* place, by letters or by visitation, he did just what he told the Ephesian elders he had done in Ephesus. He nurtured the new believers by proclaiming the whole counsel of God.

Paul, therefore, would have little use for those who advocate only a minimum of nurture from the Word on the part of the missionary. Dean Gilliland is such an example. He writes:

> While Paul was successful, above all others, in planting churches and in nurturing new Christians, he accomplished this, for the most part, by leaving neophyte Christians to seek out the answers to the questions posed by their new life. The traditional mission pattern has been for the missionary to stay, often for years, in one place, in a culture not his own, and to form the church by his own theological convictions, rather than showing the church how to think for itself. Paul would have been criticized by knowledgeable Jews for not providing a guidebook for recent converts. Instead . . . he insisted that each and every believer become an authentic Christian, able to think through the new faith and act upon it. . . . The Spirit in the life of the believer is so dynamic and transforming that missionaries ought to be able to rest from many of their worries about doctrine, morality, church growth, leadership, finances, standards, and a long list of other things that we feel must be carefully managed. . . . The written text of the Bible is certainly the supreme source of the truth. Yet, the Holy Spirit is an active and true guide in the life of every believer and we must trust him to speak directly to the regenerated human spirit.[98]

As Gilliland in Reformed fashion separates the Spirit from the Word, thus minimizing the need for thorough instruction in the Word, he sets a mission on a disaster course. Following his suggestion to let the Spirit guide apart from the Word invites another spirit into the church who is bent on destroying, not building.

As we brought out in the previous section, Paul took whatever time was necessary to nurture carefully those he had evangelized. Richard Lauersdorf emphasizes this in an essay entitled "Developing Indigenous Churches—The Scriptural Principles Involved." He writes:

> We have to ask, "Should not a fourth 'self' be added to the indigenous [self-governing, self-propagating, and self-supporting] formula? Indeed does not Scripture demand that we add a fourth?" If we want to build indigenous churches, as Scripture outlines, we must plant churches which will be not only self-governing, self-propagating, and self-supporting, but also self-disciplining. We must plant churches which know God's Word, which follow that Word in practice, and which can detect and correct departures from that Word. In short, we must sow the solid seed of the Word.[99]

Lauersdorf's suggested fourth self, self-disciplining, has been incorporated into the WELS *World Mission Handbook.* Under the heading "Self-discipline," we read:

> In order to assure a sound scriptural and evangelical practice, church planting Lutheran pastors will not be satisfied with only a vague, enthusiastic or emotional response to the proclamation of the gospel. The Savior has bid us to "Make disciples of all nations, baptizing them in the name of the Father, and of the Son and of the Holy Spirit, and teaching them to obey everything I have commanded you." . . . Missionaries strive to plant churches which know God's Word, which follow that Word in practice and which can detect and correct departures from the Word.[100]

As the handbook states, "It may take a long time to develop doctrinal awareness" to produce "an orthodox confessional Lutheran church" in a world "confused by the wooing of pseudo-Christianity."[101] But there is no shortcut to God-pleasing orthodoxy in doctrine and practice.

4. An indigenous church is self-propagating.

We have already discussed this to a certain degree in part 3 of this series under the heading "Paul's Mission Strategy"; so we will go lightly here. Paul made it quite clear that the purpose of church leaders was not just to feed the flock, although this is far from an unimportant part of their calling. Their purpose also was to train God's people for ministry so that the body of Christ might be built up, both externally and internally, as each part does its work (see Ephesians 4:11-16). Paul told Timothy: "The things you have heard me say in the presence of many witnesses entrust to reliable men who will also be qualified to teach others" (2 Timothy 2:2). A church becomes self-propagating when the taught become the teachers.

That there is always the danger of the pall of "institutionalism" settling upon the second generation church and beyond is quite clear from a reading of the letters to the seven churches of Asia Minor, especially the churches in Ephesus, Sardis, and Laodicea (Revelation 2:1-7; 3:1-6,14-22). Preservation of the institution can become the primary objective of a congregation or a church body rather than propagation of the gospel. When, quite correctly, propagation of the gospel is at the top of the agenda, then more emphasis will be placed on equipping the saints for ministry than on preserving the institution for posterity. Survival goals will give way to training for ministry goals.

We have spent some time reviewing the marvelous way that the Lord used Paul to carry out his work of spreading the gospel. Paul is unique, of course. None of us can ever hope to come close to duplicating all he was privileged to accomplish in his life. On the other hand, we do share certain privileges along with Paul. It was the Holy Spirit who converted him, called him, directed him, and encouraged him. The same Holy Spirit has done and is continuing to do the same for us.

Paul's greatest treasure was the gospel and its message of a universal reconciliation. And his treasured title was "ambassador" for the Christ who had accomplished this reconciliation. We have the same gospel of reconciliation and the same exalted title. May we, with Paul, never cease to be amazed by the gospel and to find joy and fulfillment in our calling as Christ's ambassadors.

1. Paul gives us a good example of a wise missionary. Review Paul's practices by giving one or two examples of each of the following principles Paul put into effect in his ministry.

   • Already on his first visit, Paul fed the churches "meat," not just "milk." *taught not only basic L+G, but doctrine too*

   • Paul faithfully revisited the churches he had founded.
     Lystra, Derbe, Iconium

   • Paul utilized coworkers in his nurturing work.
     Barnabas, Silas, Timothy, Mark

   • Paul nurtured his congregations through his letters.
     Kept giving them gospel

2. How do we overcome the "confirmation equals graduation" syndrome that stifles the spiritual growth of many of our members, both youth and adult? *continue to reach out + nurture them*

3. Agree or disagree: Following Paul's pattern of team ministry, it would be wise for new missions in our country to be started by two mission developers rather than one.
   yes, counsel each other, get Word out more

4. Agree or disagree: The larger the ministry team in a congregation, the less the members of a congregation tend to do.

5. In what way is the *printed* word (books, Bible studies, etc.) more valuable than the *spoken* word? How can we facilitate the production of more scripturally sound printed materials?
   —print can be referred back to + studied again
   —have qualified people write

6. Paul established indigenous churches. What does this mean?
   stand on own

7. Give examples of how Paul's churches performed for themselves the following tasks:

   • They governed themselves. *Philippi had deacons + overseers*

   • They took care of their own financial needs right from the start. *Paul felt that the churches should do this*

   • They exercised church discipline. *Paul taught elders so they could do this*

   • They spread the Word on their own, starting new congregations in the process. *the taught became the teachers*

8. Agree or disagree: A self-governing congregation is free to worship as it pleases. (The Augsburg Confession, Article VII states: "It is not necessary for the true unity of the Christian church that ceremonies, instituted by men, should be observed uniformly in all places.")

as long as doctrine is sound

9. Agree or <u>disagree</u>: "Tent-making" ministry such as Paul did should be the norm today in the church.
too many needs today

10. In his book *Missionary Methods: St. Paul's or Ours?* Roland Allen maintains that subsidizing world mission fields (1) tends to pauperize the converts and (2) tends to maintain mission unity by threats of withdrawal of financial support. Do you agree or disagree with his contention? If you agree, what is the alternative?
agree— begin with initial sum of money & let congregation know about it

11. To what degree do Roland Allen's comments above apply to the home mission field? Should home mission congregations be subsidized by the synod? What are the pluses? the minuses? What are alternatives?

12. Which is more important—nurturing the believer or extending the gospel to those who have not yet heard it?
both

13. To what degree has your congregation become a self-propagating church?

Endnotes

[1] Adolf Harnack, *The Expansion of Christianity in the First Three Centuries*, translated and edited by James Moffat, Vol. 1 (New York: G. P. Putnam's Sons, 1908), pp. 6-8.

[2] William Whiston, trans., *Josephus: The Complete Works* (Grand Rapids: Kregel Publications, 1960), XII, iii, 1.

[3] Whiston, *Josephus*, XIV, vii, 2.

[4] Harnack, *Expansion of Christianity*, pp. 17,18.

[5] Whiston, *Josephus*, XIV, x.

[6] William M. Ramsay, *St. Paul the Traveller and the Roman Citizen* (Grand Rapids: Baker Books, 1962 reprint of 1897 edition), p 33.

[7] W. J. Conybeare and J. S. Howson, *The Life and Epistles of St. Paul* (Grand Rapids: Wm. B. Eerdmans Publishing Company, 1951 edition), p. 9.

[8] Donald J. Selby, *Toward the Understanding of St. Paul* (Englewood Cliffs: Prentice Hall, 1962), p. 95.

[9] Selby, *Toward the Understanding of St. Paul*, p. 97.

[10] Roland Allen, *Missionary Methods: St. Paul's or Ours?* (Chicago: Moody Press, 1959 [first edition printed in 1912]), p. 38.

[11] Allen, *Missionary Methods*, p. 39.

[12] Brooks Alexander, "Theology from the Twilight Zone," *Christianity Today* (September 18, 1987), pp. 22-26.

[13] Harnack, *Expansion of Christianity*, p. 20, note 2.

[14] Allen, *Missionary Methods*, p. 42.

[15] Conybeare and Howson, *The Life and Epistles of St. Paul*, p. 12.

[16] Conybeare and Howson, *The Life and Epistles of St. Paul*, p. 12.

[17] E. M. Blaiklock, "Tarsus," in *The Zondervan Pictorial Encyclopedia of the Bible*, Vol. 5 (Grand Rapids: Zondervan Publishing House, 1975,1976), p. 602.

[18] F. F. Bruce, *Paul: Apostle of the Heart Set Free* (Grand Rapids: Wm. B. Eerdmans Publishing Company, 1977), p. 35.

[19] Olaf Moe, *The Apostle Paul, His Life and His Work*, translated by L. A. Vigness (Minneapolis: Augsburg Publishing House, 1950), p. 29.

[20] F. F. Bruce, *Commentary on the Book of the Acts* (Grand Rapids: Wm. B. Eerdmans Publishing Company, 1954), p. 264. Bruce mentions that Paul "as a Roman citizen must have had three names—*praenomen, nomen gentile* and *cognomen*—of which Paulus was his *cognomen.* . . . The apostle's *praenomen* and *nomen gentile,* unfortunately, have not been preserved."

[21] Pirke Aboth 2:2, as quoted in *The Zondervan Pictorial Encyclopedia of the Bible,* Vol. 4, p. 625.

[22] Whiston, *Josephus,* XIII, v, 9; XIII, x, 5.

[23] Whiston, *Josephus,* XVII, ii, 4.

[24] Whiston, *Josephus,* XIV, x, 2. Undoubtedly based on the statement "I ordain that he [the high priest] and his children retain whatever privileges belong to the office of the high priest, or whatsoever favors have been hitherto granted them."

[25] Whiston, *Josephus,* II, xx, 2; VII, viii, 7.

[26] W. C. Kaiser, Jr., "Aretas," in *The Zondervan Pictorial Encyclopedia of the Bible,* Vol. 1, p. 300.

[27] Whiston, *Josephus,* VII, iii, 3.

[28] Whiston, *Josephus,* III, xv, 3; XX, ii, 5.

[29] R. N. Longenecker, "Paul, the Apostle," in *The Zondervan Pictorial Encyclopedia of the Bible,* Vol. 4, p. 633.

[30] Reprinted in the *Wisconsin Lutheran Quarterly,* Vol. 61, No. 2 (April 1964), pp. 151-153.

[31] Conybeare and Howson, *The Life and Epistles of St. Paul,* p. 116.

[32] Ramsay, *St. Paul the Traveller,* pp. 89-97.

[33] William F. Arndt and F. Wilbur Gingrich, *A Greek-English Lexicon of the New Testament* (Chicago: University of Chicago Press, 1957), p. 442.

[34] Whiston, *Josephus,* XII, iii, 4.

[35] Ramsay, *St. Paul the Traveller,* pp. 110-112.

[36] In "Pisonem 36," in *The Expositor's Bible Commentary,* Vol. 5 (Grand Rapids: Zondervan Publishing House, 1981), pp. 470,471.

[37] See Acts 18:14-16. Gallio was the brother of the Roman philosopher, Seneca. He served as proconsul of Achaia from A.D. 51/52. A communication from the emperor Claudius to the people of Delphi mentions that Gallio was serving as proconsul of Achaia during the period of Claudius' 26th acclamation as emperor, a period known from other inscriptions to have covered the first seven months of A.D. 52. Proconsuls took office on July 1 and served for a year. Gallio could have served as proconsul, then, from A.D. 51/52 or A.D. 52/53. See *Cambridge Ancient History,* Vol. 10, p. 682.

[38] Robert Famighetti, ed., *The World Almanac and Book of Facts 1999* (Mahwah: World Almanac Books, 1998), p. 378.

[39] Famighetti, *World Almanac,* p. 862. The figures are United Nations estimates and projections and appear to be quite conservative. The fact remains that these trends denote the need to focus mission priorities on urban areas.

[40] Ramsay, *St. Paul the Traveller,* p. 72.

[41] Donald A. McGavran and Winfield C. Arn, *Ten Steps for Church Growth* (San Francisco: Harper and Row, 1977), p. 38.

[42] Donald A. McGavran, *Understanding Church Growth* (Grand Rapids: Wm. B. Eerdmans Publishing Company, revised edition, 1980), p. 75. The previous edition (1970) concerned itself only with church growth outside the United States. The revised edition applies church growth principles also to our nation. *Understanding Church Growth,* along with an earlier book by McGavran, *The Bridges of God,* are the "bibles" of the Church

Growth Movement. C. Peter Wagner writes: "Church growth is a movement rooted in Donald McGavran. . . . If you don't accept his way of looking at the Church—if you have any major conflict with *Understanding Church Growth,* our basic text—then you should use some other name because you're not part of the Church Growth Movement" (*Global Church Growth,* Vol. 22, No. 1, [January–March 1985], p. 9).

[43] C. Peter Wagner, *Your Church Can Grow* (Glendale: Regal Books, 1976), pp. 110,116.

[44] Donald A. McGavran, *The Bridges of God* (New York: Friendship Press, 1955), p. 167.

[45] McGavran, *Understanding Church Growth,* p. 406.

[46] McGavran, *Understanding Church Growth,* p. 223.

[47] McGavran, *Understanding Church Growth,* p. 230.

[48] McGavran, *Understanding Church Growth,* p. 215.

[49] McGavran, *Understanding Church Growth,* pp. 230,231.

[50] McGavran, *Understanding Church Growth,* p. 232.

[51] C. Peter Wagner, *Your Church Can Be Healthy* (Nashville: Abingdon Press, 1979), pp. 55,56.

[52] Robert G. Hoerber, "A Review of the Apostolic Council After 1925 Years," *Concordia Journal* (July 1976), pp. 158,159. His article shows how the real issue of the Jerusalem Council revolved around dealing with adiaphora in a proper way: "The Apostolic Council . . . properly makes a distinction between two matters, both of which in the New Testament era are essentially adiaphora. The distinction is proper, since some Pharisees and Judaizers are making public propaganda on the necessity of circumcision for salvation. . . . Hence the first question, on the necessity of circumcision for Christians, is no longer an adiaphoron. No compromise is possible without sacrificing doctrine. The second question concerns the eating or abstaining from certain foods traditionally objectionable to those of Jewish descent. Since no opponents are making public propaganda on this issue according to the account in Acts, the matter remains an adiaphoron. Compromise is possible and even advisable for the preservation of unity of the Church. Therefore, the Apostolic Council correctly makes a distinction between the two questions confronting the Church in A.D. 49."

[53] Waldo Werning, *The Radical Nature of Christianity* (South Pasadena: Mandate Press, a subsidiary of William Carey Library Publishers, 1975), p. 148.

[54] According to *The Win Arn Growth Report* (Pasadena: Institute for American Church Growth), No. 4, no date, but received in 1984.

[55] E. H. Wendland, "An Evaluation of Current Missiology," *Wisconsin Lutheran Quarterly,* Vol. 79, No. 3 (summer 1982), p. 179.

[56] Wendland, "An Evaluation of Current Missiology," p. 181.

[57] Allen, *Missionary Methods,* p. 47.

[58] Edgar Hoenecke, "St. Paul's Missionary Approach to the Unchurched," *Wisconsin Lutheran Quarterly,* Vol. 61, No. 2 (April 1964), p. 132.

[59] Conybeare and Howson, *The Life and Epistles of St. Paul,* p. 138.

[60] Richard N. Longenecker, *The Expositor's Bible Commentary,* Vol. 5 (Grand Rapids: Zondervan Publishing House, 1981), p. 435.

[61] This legend was retold by Ovid (around 43 B.C.–A.D. 17) in *The Metamorphoses.*

[62] The Greek literally means "a seed picker"; hence: a scavenger who prowls about the marketplace, picking up whatever scraps he can; then: a person who picks up little

scraps of knowledge and learning here and there without really understanding what he is accumulating.

[63] William Barclay puts it this way: "He knew it would be futile to talk about a history which no one knew and to quote from a book which no one had read and the authority of which no one would accept" ("A Comparison of Paul's Missionary Preaching and Preaching to the Church," in *Apostolic History and the Gospel*, Ward W. Gasque and Ralph P. Martin, eds. [Grand Rapids: Wm. B. Eerdmans Publishing Company, 1970], p. 176).

[64] "Various tales were told to account for such anonymous dedications: according to one tale, they were set up by the direction of Epimenides, a wise man of Crete, one of the poets quoted in the course of the speech. Whatever may have been the original circumstances or intention of the inscription which Paul took as his text, he interprets it as a confession of ignorance regarding the divine nature, and says that the purpose of his coming is to dispel that ignorance" (Bruce, *Paul: Apostle of the Heart Set Free*, p. 240).

[65] The Greek tragedian Euripides (around 480–406 B.C.) agreed with Paul on this, writing, "What house fashioned by builders could contain the form divine within enclosing walls?" (Bruce, *Paul: Apostle of the Heart Set Free*, p. 240).

[66] This line is also found in an earlier poem by Cleanthes (around 331–233 B.C.) entitled "Hymn to Zeus."

[67] Longenecker, *The Expositor's Bible Commentary*, p. 476.

[68] Aeschylus, "Eumenides," 647 (Bruce, *Paul: Apostle of the Heart Set Free*, p. 247).

[69] Allen, *Missionary Methods*, p. 94.

[70] Allen, *Missionary Methods*, p. 93. Sad to say, even though Allen allied himself firmly with Paul in this statement, he later "fudged" considerably by allowing for, with Zwingli, "the salvation of good heathen," p. 96.

[71] Wendland, "An Evaluation," p. 182. Time constraints prohibit us from exploring this issue more deeply. Those interested in further study of how Paul adapted his mission sermons and speeches to his audience together with an application to preaching today may be interested in a little book by Jay E. Adams, *Studies in Preaching*, Vol. 2 (Presbyterian and Reformed Publishing Company, 1976). It is subtitled "Audience Adaptations in the Sermons and Speeches of Paul." Adams writes, "Paul is the example of a healthy flexibility that Christian preaching needs for the hour; a flexibility that enables the preacher to adapt without compromise; to alter form without changing substance" (p. 68). Adams offers a 17-point checklist as an aid to analyzing the audience to which one is bringing his message and another 17-point list to assist one in adapting his message to the audience. He defines adaptation as "the speaker's ability to present the message (without over accommodation) in terms of the [audience] analysis . . . so as to achieve the immediate and/or ultimate purpose(s) for which it was delivered" (p. 2). We don't agree with Adams, by the way, when he contends that at Lystra, Paul, by rushing out, tearing his clothes, and shouting, "did not adapt and as a result lost his audience. . . . True adaptation seemingly would have called for a speech in which the audience gradually was led to understand its mistake" (p. 22). The crisis situation called for such a strong response on Paul's part.

[72] Wendland, "An Evaluation," p. 183.

[73] Thayer: "to cause a person to unite with one in a conclusion or come to the same opinion"; hence, "to prove, to demonstrate."

[74] C. Peter Wagner, ed., *Church Growth: State of the Art* (Wheaton: Tyndale House Publishers, 1986), p. 218. The book contains 22 articles written by 15 leaders in the Church Growth Movement.

[75] Wagner, *Church Growth*, pp. 223,224.

[76] For an in-depth and sound study of Pentecostals, see *A Theology of the Holy Spirit: The Pentecostal Experience and the New Testament Witness*, by Frederick Dale Bruner (Grand Rapids: Wm. B. Eerdmans Publishing Company, 1970). A good summary of the charismatic movement can be found in the essay "The Holy Spirit and the Charismatic Renewal," delivered in 1972 by Joel Gerlach to the Northern Wisconsin District Convention.

[77] Ramsay, *St. Paul the Traveller*, p. 115.

[78] Allen, *Missionary Methods*, p. 61.

[79] Carleton A. Toppe, *1 Corinthians*, of The People's Bible series (Milwaukee: Northwestern Publishing House, 1987), p. 114.

[80] David J. Valleskey, "Equipping the Believers As Disciples" in *Proceedings of the Forty-ninth Biennial Convention* (Milwaukee: Wisconsin Evangelical Lutheran Synod, 1987), p. 230.

[81] Possibly a reference to the Phrygian, or southern, section of Galatia as opposed to the original province of Galatia to the north (see also Acts 16:6).

[82] Edward F. Murphy, "The Missionary Society Is an Apostolic Team," *Missiology*, Vol. 4, No. 1 (January 1976), pp. 103-118. Murphy identifies 11 teams in the book of Acts, almost all organized by Paul.

[83] Alan Tippett, *Verdict Theology in Mission Theory* (Pasadena: William Carey Library, 1973), pp. 155-158. The author breaks down indigeneity into six components: self-image, self-functioning, self-determining, self-supporting, self-propagating, and self-giving.

[84] Allen, *Missionary Methods*, p. 105.

[85] Allen, *Missionary Methods*, p. 107.

[86] Allen, *Missionary Methods*, pp. 129-139.

[87] Allen, *Missionary Methods*, pp. 175,176.

[88] Charles Kraft, "Dynamic Equivalence Churches: An Ethnotheological Approach to Indigeneity," *Missiology*, Vol. 1, No. 1 (January 1973), pp. 39-57.

[89] E. H. Wendland, "Liturgics—Doing Their Own Thing," chapter 17 in *To Africa with Love* (Milwaukee: Northwestern Publishing House, 1974), p. 133.

[90] Roland Allen (*Missionary Methods*, pp. 26-31) argues unsuccessfully that Paul's synagogue connection did not give him any real advantage over missionaries today: "When we take it for granted, as we so often do, that the existence of a synagogue and the presence of some God-fearing Greeks in a city so alter the problem of Church building that methods used by St. Paul under these circumstances cannot possibly be applied to any modern conditions, I think we are labouring under a delusion."

[91] Allen, *Missionary Methods*, pp. 65-81.

[92] Allen, *Missionary Methods*, p. 69.

[93] Allen, *Missionary Methods*, p. 70.

[94] The other six reasons advanced by Allen for not providing outside funding for a mission (*Missionary Methods*, pp. 70-78) are as follows: (1) A church from a foreign country seeking permanent holdings in a mission field may arouse the opposition of the country in which it is working. (2) Missionaries get loaded down with secular business, for example, negotiations with contractors and management of property, which keeps them from their real work. (3) It misrepresents a church's purpose for coming to a place. (Allen: "By importing an institution we tend to obscure the truly spiritual character of our work.") (4) Missionaries get tied down to one place. With so much money invested in property and buildings, they can't easily move, and so they cease to be evangelists and become pas-

tors. (5) It makes it difficult for a native to succeed the missionary, because he doesn't enjoy all the advantages of the missionary, especially his ability to raise money. (6) Problems arise later in turning the property over to the native church.

[95] Allen, *Missionary Methods*, p. 75.

[96] Allen, *Missionary Methods*, p. 75.

[97] Allen, *Missionary Methods*, p. 116.

[98] Dean S. Gilliland, *Pauline Theology and Mission Practice* (Grand Rapids: Baker Books, 1983), pp. 34,124,127.

[99] This paper was read at the June 1979 WELS World Missionaries Conference held at Leland, Michigan. The quotation is from page 5 of the paper.

[100] Published in 1987 by the WELS Board for World Missions. The quotation is from Section 4, "Church Planting," p. 3.

[101] "Church Planting," p. 4.